# The American War of Independence 1775-83

Allan Ramsay, Portrait of George III, *c.* 1767

# The American War of Independence 1775-83

A COMMEMORATIVE EXHIBITION
ORGANIZED BY THE MAP LIBRARY AND
THE DEPARTMENT OF MANUSCRIPTS
OF THE BRITISH LIBRARY
REFERENCE DIVISION

4 July to 11 November 1975

Published for
THE BRITISH LIBRARY
by British Museum Publications Limited

© 1975, *The British Library Board*
ISBN  0 7141 0377 2 *Cased*
          0 7141 0378 0 *Paper*
*Published by British Museum Publications Ltd*
*6 Bedford Square, London* WC1B 3RA
*Designed by Brian Paine*
*Set in Monotype Garamond* 156
*Printed in Great Britain by*
*Balding & Mansell Ltd, London and Wisbech*

# Foreword

The War of Independence, in which the American colonists defeated the armies of King George III, began in 1775. The present exhibition is the first in a series of events planned to celebrate the Declaration of Independence in 1776. Only the British would take so much trouble over the bicentenary of an humiliating defeat. Present-day anti-imperialists may see a guilty conscience in what we are doing. They would be wrong. We are not offering an apology for colonizing the eastern parts of the United States. We are putting on record our satisfaction that the War did not kill the friendship between America and Britain. We like each other well, and have served the world better because, after a sharp domestic quarrel, we agreed to a divorce.

Consider the triumphant position of Britain in 1775. We had just turned the French out of Canada and India. Australia and New Zealand were waiting for settlers. It was asking a lot of our rulers to recognise that their power was overstretched and ought to be shared with the thirteen colonies in North America. All the more remarkable that many of the best minds in Britain did see that the rebels were in the right.

In those days, when liberty was at stake, feeling ran high, and in this exhibition we show the quarrel smouldering to flash point, followed by the ups and downs of the War, the making of peace, and all through evidence on both sides that blood is thicker than water and that personal friendships were not going to be broken.

The exhibition is arranged in the famous library built to contain the books which King George III had himself collected. Many of the items on show come from this Royal Library and from other collections in the British Library and from the Department of Prints and Drawings and other departments of the British Museum. The Board of The British Library is grateful to Her Majesty the Queen for the loan of a fine drawing and of two letters of King George III. We are also indebted to the Duke of Northumberland for his ancestor's papers which have not been seen in public before, and for other loans which are recorded in Dr Helen Wallis' Introduction to the catalogue. The King never saw the room built to contain his books. But then he never saw the ex-colonists from the United States twice cross the Atlantic to fight with us for freedom.

ECCLES
*Chairman of the Board of the British Library*

# Contents

# Introduction

The collections of the British Library and of the British Museum form the nucleus of this exhibition commemorating the American War of Independence. These are supplemented by the loan of important pieces from public and private collections in Great Britain. The history of the War on the North American continent is told by means of a wide range of contemporary materials, graphic and documentary. Maps and views recreate the scenes of battle and illustrate the planning of campaigns. Letters and reports document the sequence of military and political events. The play of public opinion and the political controversies surrounding the War are reflected in a wealth of publications, comprising books, pamphlets, newspaper articles and cartoons.

## Maps and views

The great library of King George III built up during the sixty years of his reign, and presented to the British Museum by King George IV, included a topographical and geographical collection which ranked as the finest of its day. It is rich in maps and views illustrating the Seven Years War, 1756–63, (known in America as the French and Indian Wars), the period of imperial consolidation and incipient conflict, 1763–75, and the War of Independence, 1775–83. In the centuries before photography the military had a prime need for accurate draughtsmanship, not only in map-making and surveying, but also in topographical depiction. The Royal Military Academy at Woolwich which trained artillery and engineer officers for the British Army also taught topographical drawing. Its chief drawing-master from 1768 to 1799 was Paul Sandby, 'the Father of the English School of water colour'. England's lead in watercolour painting is thus reflected in the fine topographical drawings made by men like Thomas Davies, Henry Gilder and James Peachey who served as army officers in North America. Henry Gilder, whose drawing of the Naval squadron on Lake Champlain, 1776, is preserved in the Royal Library at Windsor Castle, was a pupil of Paul's brother, Thomas Sandby, and already exhibiting at the Royal Academy. This drawing (no. 81) has been graciously lent by Her Majesty the Queen. Bernard Ratzer's Plan of the City of New York, 1770, with its accompanying view (no. 103) is an example of detailed topographical survey in one of the best mapped areas of colonial America. The watercolour view of Boston in 1775 gives an eye-witness impression of what it was like to be a red-coat standing on the ramparts overlooking the besieged city (no. 58). Foremost in political importance is John Mitchell's map of North America, 1775, annotated by the British peace commissioner, Richard Oswald, to show the boundary of the United States of America, as agreed in the Preliminary Articles of Peace, 30 November 1782 (no. 176). Described as the most important map in North American history, the red-lined map (as it is known) has been called in evidence in nearly every subsequent boundary dispute affecting American territory.

The general collections of the Map Library and the Department of Manuscripts are also rich in maps and topographical material relating to the War. The map of the cantonments of His Majesty's Forces in North America, 1766 (no. 6), illustrating the transfer of troops from the interior to the Atlantic colonies, a major cause of dispute between provincial assemblies and the British Government, is on view for the first time. A major acquisition of recent years, the Royal United Service Institution's Map Collection, purchased in 1968, includes eighteenth century MS and printed American maps derived primarily from the collections of Lord Amherst, Commander-in-Chief of the British Forces in the Seven Years War, and of Colonel Sir Augustus Frazer who in 1827 probably acquired his collection as Inspector of the Ordnance Carriage Department at Woolwich. The first published plan of Bunker Hill, 1775 (no. 51), Henry Pelham's map of Boston 1777 (no. 67), and the MS plan of General Burgoyne's camp near Stillwater, 1777 (no. 87), illustrate the resources of the RUSI Collection, which supplements the King's Topographical Collection.

Many of the maps made for the commanding officers, notably Generals Gage and Clinton, remained in private hands and were subsequently acquired by the William L. Clements Library in the USA. In Great Britain the private collections of His Grace the Duke of Northumberland include a fine set of maps brought home by his ancestor Lord Percy, who served as Colonel under Gage in the Boston campaigns. From these His Grace has kindly lent five MS maps and plans. Two sketch maps depict the opening scenes of battle in and about Boston (nos. 47, 48). The work of C. J. Sauthier, Lord Percy's secretary and surveyor, is represented by two MS topographical surveys of Newport and New York (nos. 119, 115), while the fifth is one of a series of battle plans by G. E. Barron (no. 141).

*Manuscript and printed sources*

Of the many books and manuscripts preserved in the King's Library associated with the War one of the most interesting is General Simcoe's *Journal of the Operations of the Queen's Rangers* [1787], annotated with notes and watercolour drawings and presented to the King by the author with the accompanying proposal that one of His Majesty's sons should be at the head of a recommended new light Corps of Rangers (no. 149). Simcoe was later to present to the King the fine birch-bark drawings of Upper Canada executed by his wife while he was undertaking his duties as Governor of the new province where the American loyalists were resettled (no. 199). Collections of political papers have yielded valuable documents relevant to the War and the making of peace. These include the papers of Caleb Whitefoord, Secretary to the British peace commission, whose long friendship with Benjamin Franklin contributed to the bond of goodwill between the British and American negotiators at Paris (no. 179). Letters and communiqués concerning the implementation of the peace terms in North America, among them a letter from George

Washington (no. 192), are selected from the papers of General Haldimand, Commander-in-Chief in Canada 1778–85. The Philatelic Branch of the British Library has provided from the Archives of the Inland Revenue the Register of the Stamp Duty Dies, one of only two copies known (no. 3).

To illustrate the major political events in the background to the War and the negotiations for peace three items have been borrowed from the Public Record Office, by kind permission of the Lord Chancellor: the Petition of the First Continental Congress (no. 39), the Preliminary Articles of Peace between Great Britain and America, 1782 (no. 169), and the Declaration of the Cessation of Hostilities in the United States, 15 April 1783 (no. 174). A series of cartoons borrowed from the Department of Prints and Drawings of the British Museum provide satirical commentary on the activities of the belligerent powers and the individual actors in the drama of war and peace-making. Two letters of King George III graciously lent by Her Majesty the Queen (no. 186), show how deeply the King felt the loss of America: 'I think this compleats the Downfall of the lustre of this Empire'. A letter of Lord Cornwallis written shortly after the surrender of Yorktown is kindly lent by Mr Thomas Tesoriero of New York (no. 164).

### Portraits and memorabilia

The Antiquities Departments of the British Museum have kindly lent, in addition to the cartoons, various portraits, medallions, and commemorative medals. From the Department of Medieval and Later Antiquities comes an exquisite porcelain figurine of William Pitt, Earl of Chatham (no. 8), who stands as America's champion, protecting an American Indian kneeling beside him. 'I rejoice that America has resisted' he had declared. Official and private collections have also lent a variety of two and three-dimensional objects. The portrait of King George III by Allan Ramsay (no. 1), is borrowed from the Guildhall Library. The National Army Museum has provided a miniature of Sir Henry Clinton (no. 128), an oil painting of the Burial of Simon Fraser (no. 88), and contemporary uniforms. From the Armouries of the Tower of London come firearms and swords, together with a powder horn engraved with a map of the Mohawk and Hudson rivers (no. 92), and from the National Portrait Gallery portraits and a medallion. Stanley Gibbons Currency Ltd. has lent a set of American bank notes. The Ferguson rifle, c.1776, from Mr W. Keith Neal, is of particular interest, as an invention designed to meet the challenge of rapid fire from American backwoodsmen and sharp shooters (no. 144).

### Acknowledgements

For their generous consent to the loan of items in the Museum collections the British Library Board wishes to express its thanks to the Director and Trustees of the British Museum and to the Keepers of the Department of Prints and Drawings, of Medieval and Later Antiquities, and of Coins and Medals. The Board also expresses its deep appreciation of the loans of the various items in public and private collections, as noted above. In acknowledging the gracious consent of Her Majesty the Queen to the loan of the Gilder drawing and the letters of King George III, thanks are also due to Her Majesty's Librarian, Mr Robert Mackworth Young and to the Curator of the Print Room, Miss Jane Low. The kindness of His Grace the Duke of Northumberland in lending the five maps is much appreciated, and also the help of Mr D. P. Graham, Surveyor of the Northumberland Estates.

To fill gaps in the narrative, photographs have been obtained from America, notably the Connecticut Historical Society, the Massachusetts Historical Society, the Independence National Historical Park Collection, and the Henry Francis du Pont Winterthur Museum. In Great Britain the Viscount Gage has kindly provided a photograph of his ancestor General Gage. Thanks are also due to T. R. Adams, Director of the John Carter Brown Library for making available the typescript of his forthcoming book *The American Controversy. A Chronological Short-title List of the . . . pamphlets published in Great Britain 1765–1783 relating to her American Colonies*; and to Professor W. P. Cumming for the use of his inventory of the maps at Alnwick Castle, now published in *Maps of British Colonial America* (1974). Professor and Mrs Cumming also gave valuable advice, notably on the graphic documentation of the War, undertaken in preparation for Professor Cumming's book written in collaboration with Hugh Rankin for the Phaidon Press, *The Fate of a Nation*. Kenneth Nebenzahl's kindness in making available the typescript of his forthcoming *Bibliography of Contemporary Printed Maps of the American Revolutionary War* is also appreciated.

The exhibition, which has been organized jointly by the Map Library of the Department of Printed Books and by the Department of Manuscripts, is designed to illustrate the strength of the Library's collections and to interest the layman and the scholar alike. Opening with the 'War of words, 1763–1775', it depicts the campaigns in the main theatres of war on the American continent and concludes with the Peace Treaty signed at Paris in 1783. For the various sections of the exhibition and of the catalogue, the following officers have been responsible: Section I – Sarah Tyacke; Sections II and V – Yolande O'Donoghue; Section III – Hugh Cobbe; Section IV – Robert Smith; Section VI – Helen Wallis. Acknowledgement is also due to E. J. Miller and David Jarvis for help with official publications, and to John Barr, Exhibitions Officer of the Department of Printed Books, for useful activities of liaison with the British Museum. Richard Fowler and Linda Stoddart of the Design Office of the British Museum have been responsible for the design of the exhibition. George Miles (Map Library) and Victor Carter (Department of Manuscripts Conservation Officer) have undertaken the mounting of graphic items. E. C. Jones of the Map Library and Shelley Jones of the Department of Manuscripts have handled the routines of organization.

HELEN WALLIS
*Map Librarian*

# 1 *The War of Words: Great Britain and America* 1764–75

For His Majesty's Ministers the acquisition of vast French territories in America, by the Treaty of Paris 1763, posed new administrative problems, which forced the thirteen colonies into Parliament's reluctant view. An aristocratic and factious assembly, Parliament concerned itself but intermittently with American affairs, often willing to accept any solution to the problem of financing the defence of colonial frontiers which would relieve the British taxpayer. Unlike the East India Company 'nabobs', the colonists had no substantial representation in Parliament and had to rely on vociferous but distant complaint to thwart legislation. The distance between Great Britain and America also tended to obscure the realities of a complex but casual colonial system which had served both countries to their mutual contentment. As Edmund Burke remarked: 'Seas roll and months pass between the order and the execution.'

After 1763 successive ministries determined to control the American continent more effectively, and to raise money in the colonies by a series of measures considered novel and provocative by their opponents. The Stamp Act (1765), Townshend's Duties, the setting up of a Board of Customs Commissioners (1767), and finally the Tea Act (1773), all caused resistance and riot in America and contributed to the steady accumulation of distrust and antagonism between Great Britain and the colonies. By the end of 1774 the two sides were set rigidly against each other.

Accompanying British action was an ever-increasing insistence on parliamentary supremacy, admirably stated in the English political bible, Sir William Blackstone's *Commentaries on the Laws of England* (1765): 'There is and must be in every state a supreme irresistible, absolute, and uncontrollable authority in which . . . the rights of sovereignty reside; this supreme power is by the constitution of Great Britain vested in King, Lords and Commons.' Parliamentary omnicompetence was not to go unchallenged in America; nor in England, where the career of John Wilkes, William Pitt's refusal to admit Parliament's right to tax the unrepresented colonies, and Edmund Burke's advocacy of pragmatism in American affairs, revealed the constant desire of some to preserve the Empire peacefully. 'I am resolved this day,' said Burke on 22 March 1775, 'to have nothing at all to do with the question of the right of taxation. The question with me, is not whether you have a right to render your people [i.e. Americans] miserable; but whether it is not your interest to make them happy.'

Like many American colonists in 1763, the Reverend Samuel Cooper of Boston looked forward to 'a lasting peace . . . our settlements extending themselves with security on Every Side, changing a wilderness into a fruitful Field'. Instead the colonists found themselves prohibited by the British army from expanding westward beyond the Alleghenies, and their colonial 'liberties' attacked by successive Acts of Parliament. Opposition, both from radicals and later loyalists, crystallized round the issue of taxation, and gradually widened to encompass matters of constitutional principle. While the Loyalists drew back from overturning that 'firm Loyalty to the Crown and faithful Adherence to the Government', as Benjamin Franklin expressed it in

1765, 'which is the Safety as well as the Honour of the Colonies', Samuel Adams, James Otis, Patrick Henry and John Hancock thought otherwise. By 1773 the Royal Governor of Massachusetts, Thomas Hutchinson, was maintaining that, 'no line can be drawn between the supreme Authority of Parliament and the total Independence of the colonies', and the American opposition were ready to argue that 'if there can be no such line, the Consequence is either that the Colonies are the vassals of Parliament, or that they are totally Independent. As it cannot be supposed that we should be reduced to a state of Vassalage, the Conclusion is . . . that we were thus Independent', a viewpoint promoted and maintained by organizations such as the 'Sons of Liberty' and the Committees of Correspondence between colony and colony. When British attitudes hardened after the Boston Tea Party in 1773 the colonists were therefore not unprepared. They called the First Continental Congress in September 1774, where the machinery for united colonial action against Great Britain was established, and the means for waging war, if necessary, anticipated.

## British politicians and America 1764–75

### 1 George III (1738–1820)

Portrait by Allan Ramsay c.1767

3 × 2m

*Lent by the Guildhall Library*

Allan Ramsay (1713–84) son of the Scottish poet was introduced to George III then Prince of Wales by Lord Bute, the Prince's hated but influential adviser. In 1767 Ramsay was appointed Painter in Ordinary to George III and founded an establishment which specialized in producing portraits of George III and his Queen. The portrait (frontispiece) was presented to the Corporation of the City of London by George III.

### 2 The Stamp Act, 1765

'An Act for granting and applying certain stamp duties. . . in America.'

*BL Official Publications, Library General Public Acts Anno septimo Georgii III Regis Cap. XI*

'In what mode', wrote Lord Egremont, Secretary of State to the Board of Trade, in May 1763, 'least Burthensome and most palatable to the Colonies, can they contribute toward the support of the Additional Expense, which must attend their Civil and Military Establishment?' Proposed as early as 1742, the exaction of stamp duty on legal and other enumerated papers in America, as in England, presented itself to the Treasury as a welcome means of raising revenue. Its political implications were as evident to Grenville's ministry as they were to the colonists. Thomas Whateley, joint secretary to the Treasury, declared in 1765: 'The great Measure of the Sessions, is the American Stamp Act; I give it the appelation of a *great measure* on account of the important point it established, the Right of Parliament to lay an internal Tax upon the Colonies.' The Act, effective from 1 November 1765, levied stamp duties on a wide range of legal and commercial documents.

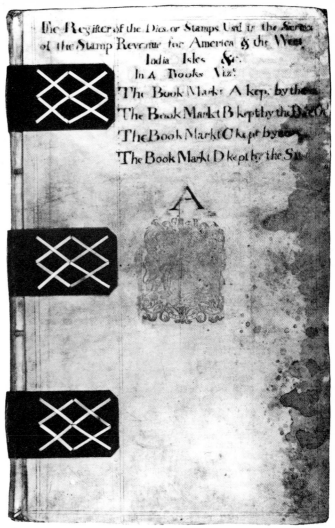

3

### 3 The Stamp Duty Register

The Register of the Dies or Stamps used in the service of the Stamp Revenue for America and West Indies Isles &c. Book A.

46cm

*BL Philatelic Section, Inland Revenue Archives, List I, Book 2*

Kept by the then Secretary to the Commissioners of Stamps, this Register contains examples of the dies impressed on to paper, issued for the printing of legal and commercial documents listed in the Stamp Act. Only two such registers were ever compiled; the other was held by the Supervisor of the Stamping Department and remains in the collections of the Inland Revenue.

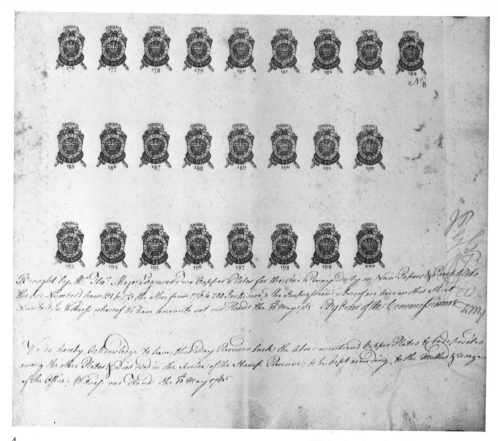

4

## 4 Stamp Duty Stamps

A sheet of proof 1d stamp duties for newspapers. 10 May 1765.

20 × 25 cm

*BL Philatelic Section, Inland Revenue Archives, List 6, Book 3, sh. 35*

Pursuant to the Stamp Act the Commissioners of Stamps authorized designs of the various values of stamps to be stamped on to papers used for the printing of the many legal and commercial documents listed in the Act. Those shown indicate the penny duty payable on all pamphlets and papers 'being larger than half a sheet and not exceeding one whole sheet'. The proofs were submitted by the engraver to the Commissioners for their approval on 10 May 1765.

## 5 The Difficulties of an American Stamp Distributor, 1766

Letter from Jared Ingersoll, to the Governor of the Colony of New York. Dated 3 January 1766.

MS, autograph. 21 × 17 cm

*BL Department of Manuscripts Add. MS 22679. f.8*

With the legal obligation to print many documents on the stamped paper, the Stamp Commissioners had acquired a virtual monopoly of the sale of much of the paper in the colonies. Furthermore documents requiring stamps, if not stamped were inadmissible as evidence in any court; heavy penalties were incurred by any public official or lawyer proceeding in any suit without them, and on persons selling unstamped newspapers, almanacs, pamphlets or cards.

The violent reaction which the application of the Act provoked soon resulted in the resignation of many of the distributors, including Jared Ingersoll, distributor for Connecticut. On his arrival at New Haven from England he was met by 'about Five Hundred Men, all on horseback carrying pretty long and large new-made white staves'. Under such pressure it is hardly surprising that he thought it prudent to write to Sir Henry Moore, Governor of the Colony of New York asking him to 'receive into the fort and protect in the best manner you are able the stampt papers . . . the late tumults and violences here [New Haven] having prevented me from being able to receive them agreeable to the directions of the commissioners'.

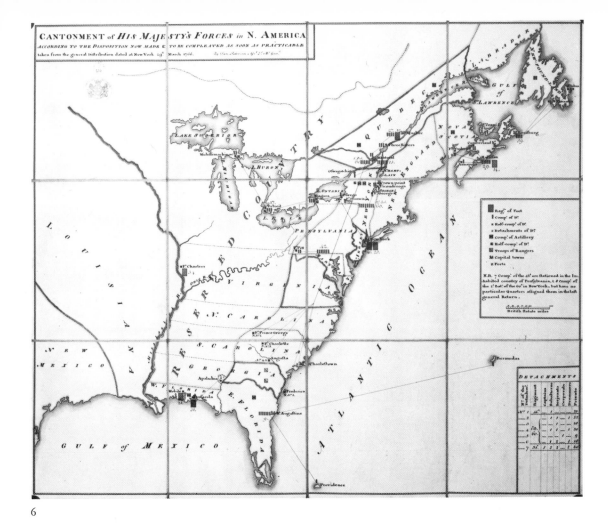

## 6 British Troops in North America

Cantonment of His Majesty's Forces in N. America according to the disposition now made & to be compleated as soon as practicable taken from the general Distribution dated at New York 29th March 1766. By Dan. Paterson Asst. Qr. Mr. Genl.

1:375,000 approx. 54 × 60cm

*BL Department of Manuscripts Add. MS 11288*

At the end of the Seven Years' War fifteen regiments, about 6,000 British troops in all, were stationed in North America where they were employed policing the newly acquired French and Spanish territories, and pacifying and protecting the Indians of the interior. During the Stamp Act crisis, 1765–66, Thomas Gage, Commander-in-Chief in North America, began to withdraw troops to the Atlantic colonies, with the evident intention of using military force to support civil rule. As he wrote to Secretary Conway on 22 February 1766; 'When I see the King's Affairs in such a situation . . . I must take my own Resolution; which is to draw all the Force I can, and as soon as it can be done into the Provinces. . . . A New Disposition must be made of the Troops to answer the purposes intended. . .' The new disposition was sent to London on 28 March, from which Ensign Daniel Paterson (1738–1825), later well known for his roadbooks and itineraries, made this map. Troops were withdrawn from all but the largest forts in the interior, and quartered on the unwilling colonists in the provinces of New York and Pennsylvania. The garrisons at Halifax, Nova Scotia and Quebec, within easy reach of dissident colonies, were also reinforced. Both payment for the troops and their presence in the older colonies became a continual source of dispute between provincial assemblies and the British Government.

THE REPEAL. *or the Funeral Procession, of MISS AMERIC-STAMP.*

7

### 7 The Repeal of the Stamp Act, 1766

The Repeal, or the Funeral Procession, of Miss Americ-Stamp.

17 × 37cm

*BM Department of Prints and Drawings, Satires 4140*

An engraving of the bank of the Thames, with warehouses in the background; one of which is inscribed 'The Sheffield and Birmingham Warehouse Goods now ship'd for America'. Three ships float in the river, named after His Majesty's ministers, Grafton, Rockingham and Conway. On the quay are two large bales, one of which is labelled 'Stamps from America'. A procession approaches the tomb with George Grenville, chief minister and First Lord of the Treasury, sometimes called the 'Stamper', carrying a little child's coffin for: 'Miss Americ Stamp born 1765 died 1766.'

### 8 America's Champion

A porcelain figure of William Pitt, Earl of Chatham (1708–78). Probably attributable to Derby. Painted in colours with gilding.

Height: 13in, 33cm

*BM Department of Medieval and Later Antiquities Porcelain catalogue II.48*

Thought to have been made on Pitt's elevation to an earldom in 1766, the figure shows Pitt, his arm resting on a pedestal, inscribed 'Wm Pitt, Earl of Chatham', protecting an American Indian kneeling beside him. His memorable speech on 14 January 1766 commending the American colonists' refusal to submit to taxation imposed by the Stamp Act of 1765 no doubt inspired the figure. 'I rejoice that America has resisted,' declared Pitt, but he also emphasized the power of Parliament to legislate for the colonies 'that we

68

8

81

may bind their trade, confine their manufactures, and exercise every power whatsoever, except that of taking their money out of their pocket without their consent'.

In 1770 a statue was erected to Pitt on Wall Street, New York 'as a public testimony . . . to the many eminent services he rendered America, particularly in promoting the Repeal of the Stamp Act'. For Colour Plate, see p. 19.

### 9 William Pitt, Earl of Chatham (1708–78)

Oval medallion: the head is in profile facing left, on a blue ground.

Impressed mark on the back:
WEDGWOOD & BENTLEY

Height: 3½in, 10cm

Modelled by John Flaxman Jr, 1778

*BM Department of Medieval and Later Antiquities 1919–3–5, 4*

### 10 Charles Townshend (1725–67)

Wax medallion. Artist Isaac Gossett.

12 × 9cm

*Lent by the National Portrait Gallery*

Chancellor of the Exchequer in William Pitt's last ministry, Townshend was noted both for his brilliant oratory and for his capricious and high-handed ways. On taking office, 'he pledged himself', in the Duke of Grafton's words, 'contrary to the known decision of every member of the Cabinet, to draw a certain revenue from the colonies without offence to the Americans themselves'. He introduced a bill to raise colonial import duties and another for the establishment of American Commissioners of Customs to enforce the Act. Townshend did not live to see the protest he provoked, dying of a 'neglected fever' on 4 September 1767.

10

### 11 Raising Revenue, 1767

An Act for granting certain Duties in the British Colonies and Plantations in America; . . . and for more effectually preventing the clandestine Running of Goods in the said Colonies and Plantations.

*BL Official Publications Library, General Public Acts, Anno septimo Georgii III Regis Cap. XLVI*

No doubt through illness, Pitt raised no objection to the introduction of Townshend's Act 'for defraying the charge of the Administration of Justice, and the Support of Civil Government, in such Provinces where it shall be found necessary; and towards further defraying the Expenses of defending, protecting and securing the said Dominions' in America. Hoping to raise £40,000 by imposing duties on glass, red and white lead, painters' colours, paper and tea, the ministry found that between 1767 and 1769 total revenue from the American colonies was £28,904. 17s. 8¾d, while the cost of collection was £16,430. 7s. 1d. With some relief Lord North's government repealed the duties in 1770 but retained them, as a matter of principle, for tea.

( 655 )

Anno septimo

# Georgii III. Regis.

### C A P. XLVI.

An Act for granting certain Duties in the *British* Colonies and Plantations in *America*; for allowing a Drawback of the Duties of Customs upon the Exportation, from this Kingdom, of Coffee and Cocoa Nuts of the Produce of the said Colonies or Plantations; for discontinuing the Drawbacks payable on China Earthen Ware exported to *America*; and for more effectually preventing the clandestine Running of Goods in the said Colonies and Plantations.

 WHEREAS it is expedient that a Revenue should be raised, in Your Majesty's Dominions in America, for making a more certain and adequate Provision for defraying the Charge of the Administration of Justice, and the Support of Civil Government, in such Provinces where it shall be found necessary; and towards further defraying the Expences of defending, protecting, and securing, the said Dominions; We, Your Majesty's most dutiful and loyal Subjects, the Commons of Great Britain, in Parliament assembled, have therefore resolved to give and grant unto Your Majesty the several Rates

8 C 2 and

b

11

BL *Official Publications Library, General Public Acts Anno septimo Georgii III Regis Cap. XLI*

Much of Townshend's plan for raising revenue in America rested upon strict enforcement of the trade laws to combat smuggling estimated at a loss to the Treasury of £500,000. 'The principal Articles Smuggled into North America', wrote Gage to Lord Shelburne, Secretary of State in 1766, 'are several sorts of Dutch East-India Goods, particularly Teas in great Quantitys, Spices, Chintzes, *etc.*, Dutch Gun-Powder, German Linnens, Hemp, Yarn, *etc.*' Customs Commissioners, each paid an annual salary of £500, to avoid being 'dependent upon the pleasure of any Assembly', were appointed to Boston in 1767, to control customs at ports from St John's, Newfoundland, to Mobile in West Florida. Giving them judicial support were the reorganized vice-admiralty courts which dealt speedily with any trade or revenue cases at Halifax, Boston, Philadelphia or Charleston. Court procedure differed markedly from common law courts. A single judge heard and determined all cases, with no jury present. Goods or ships seized were the property of the crown unless the owner could prove his innocence at his own expense. If the goods were confiscated the provincial governor, the customs officer, and the Revenue each received one-third of their value. By 1769 the vice-admiralty courts' extensive powers as adjuncts to the customs service were bitterly resented by colonial merchants.

## 12 The Customs Commissioners, 1767

An Act to enable His Majesty to put the Customs, and other Duties, in the British Dominions in America, and the Execution of the Laws relating to Trade there, under the Management of Commissioners to be appointed for that Purpose, and to be resident in the said Dominions.

## 13 A Customs Officer's Warrant, 1767

[Begin:] To all people to whom these presents shall come we the Commissioners for managing & causing to be levied his Majesty's Customs ... Do hereby Depute and Impower [       ] By virtue whereof He hath power to enter into any Ship, Bottom Boat or other Vessel ... there to make diligent search ... for any Goods, Wares, or Merchandizes, prohibited ...

43 × 33cm

*BL Department of Printed Books Tab.580.b.1*

Typical of the many clashes between the commissioners of customs and colonial merchants was the episode involving John Hancock's sloop *Liberty*. In May 1768 a customs official Thomas Kirk boarded the vessel in Boston harbour and was, according to his own testimony, forced below deck while the cargo was landed at night. The sloop was seized and placed under the guard of HMS *Rodney*'s guns in the harbour, while Hancock was charged with importing Madeira wine which he had failed to declare. John Adams (later to draw up the Declaration of Independence) defended Hancock in the vice-admiralty court, questioning the court's competence and even that of Parliament to legislate and tax the colonists. In the spring of 1769 the prosecution was dropped, but not before the Governor had requested the stationing of three regiments of soldiers in the town to ensure enforcement of the recent Acts of Parliament.

## 14 Wilkes and Liberty

John Wilkes Esq. Drawn from the Life and Etch'd in Aquafortis by William Hogarth.

Published 16 May 1763.

32 × 22cm

*BM Department of Prints and Drawings, Satires 4050*

The antagonism felt by Americans, in the decade before the War of Independence, against 'arbitrary government' was mirrored in England by the celebrated activities of John Wilkes (1727–97). In April 1763 Wilkes was accused of printing a seditious libel in his newspaper the *North Briton*, issue no. 45, where he attacked the Treaty of Paris. A general warrant was issued to arrest the 'authors printers and publishers' of this work. Wilkes was committed to the Tower but as an MP he was discharged on grounds of

14

privilege. He then successfully brought an action for damages against the officers who had ransacked his house and office. His success soon turned sour when he was expelled from the Commons and outlawed for his continuing seditious activities. He was lauded as a martyr in the American colonies, where the Sons of Liberty at Boston and elsewhere repeatedly raised the toast 'Wilkes and Liberty'.

( 895 )

ANNO DECIMO TERTIO

# Georgii III. Regis.

C A P. XLIV.

An Act to allow a Drawback of the Duties of Customs on the Exportation of Tea to any of His Majesty's Colonies or Plantations in *America*; to increase the Deposit on Bohea Tea to be sold at the *India Company*'s Sales; and to impower the Commissioners of the Treasury to grant Licences to the *East India Company* to export Tea Duty-free.

 WHEREAS by an Act, made in the Preamble. Twelfth Year of His present Majesty's Reign, (intituled, An Act for granting a Drawback of Part of the Customs upon the Exportation of Tea to *Ireland*, and the *British* Dominions in *America*; for altering the Drawback upon foreign Sugars exported from *Great Bri-*    10 R 2    tain

16

---

## 15 The Sons of Liberty

Letter to John Wilkes Esq., in King's Bench Prison from the Committee of the Sons of Liberty in the Town of Boston. Dated 6th June, 1768.

30 × 15cm

*BL Department of Manuscripts,*
*Add. MS 30870.f.45*

Provoked by the Stamp Act of 1765, groups of 'considerable and respectable' men formed associations to combat the law, calling themselves the 'Sons of Liberty'. General Gage blamed New York's riots on them, for 'nothing Publick is Transacted without them. . . . The whole Body of Merchants in general, Assembly Men, Magistrates, &c. have been united in this Plan of Riots. . . . The Sailors who are the only People who may be properly stiled Mob are entirely at the command of the Merchants who employ them.' After repeal of the Act, the Sons maintained their vigilance enlisting support where they could, notably from John Wilkes in England, praying that his 'perseverance in the good old cause may still prevent the great System from dashing to pieces'. As a gift they sent him a copy of John Dickinson's *Letters from a Farmer*: 'We humbly present you the Farmer his sentiments are ours' (see no. 28).

## 16 Government Assistance to the East India Company, 1773

An Act to allow a Drawback of the Duties of Customs on the Exportation of Tea to any of His Majesty's Colonies or Plantations in America . . .

*BL Official Publications Library, General Public Acts Anno decimo tertio Georgii III Regis Cap. XLIV.*

In 1773 the East India Company, near bankruptcy, petitioned the Government for financial assistance. As part of an overall plan to save the company, it was allowed to export tea, wholesale and free of duties, to the British colonies and there auction the tea through appointed agents, in direct competition with the traders in smuggled foreign teas. The American duty of 3*d* per lb on

18

tea remained, but the Government's hope was, as Benjamin Franklin noted, that the scheme would 'take off so much Duty here [in England], as will make tea cheaper in America than Foreigners can supply us, and to confine the Duty there [in America] to keep up the Exercise of Right [of taxing the colonies]'. The point was not lost on the colonial merchants, whose business interests merged with the defence of principle, when they realized that the East India Company would obtain a virtual monopoly of the tea trade in America if they did not oppose the Act. The first batch of monopoly tea to arrive was dumped in Boston harbour on 16 December 1773 (see no. 37 for an eye-witness account).

## 17 Retaliation for the Boston Tea Party

An Act to discontinue, in such Manner, and for such Time as are therein mentioned, the landing and discharging, lading or shipping, of Goods, Wares and Merchandise, at the Town, and within the Harbour, of Boston, in the Province of Massachusetts Bay, in North America.

*BLL Official Publications Library, General Public Acts Anno decimo quarto Georgii III Regis Cap. XIX*

On 7 March 1774 George III requested members of Parliament to empower him to take 'such measures as would stop the violent and outrageous Proceedings at the Town and Port of Boston . . . and for better securing the Execution of the Laws, and the just Dependence of the Colonies upon the Crown and Parliament of Great Britain'. By June four coercive bills had been passed: the Customs house at Boston was to be removed to Marblehead and ships prohibited from unloading in Boston harbour; the provincial constitution altered to ensure that the governor's council was composed of crown appointees and that no town meetings were held without the governor's written permission; at the governor's discretion, persons indicted of capital offences while carrying out official duties, were to be tried, not, as was customary, by their

neighbours, but in courts outside the province; in the case of civil disturbance, quarters for the military were to be provided by the townspeople, not, as hitherto, at Castle William. Attempting to explain the absence of protest in England to the New York assembly in April, Edmund Burke wrote: 'The Popular current, both within doors [of Parliament] and without, at present sets strangely against America . . . such is the temper of Parliament and of the Nation at this moment.' To implement the Acts directed against Massachusetts Bay, a military Governor, General Thomas Gage was appointed to replace the unfortunate Thomas Hutchinson.

## 18 A Military Governor for Massachusetts

Thomas Gage by J. Meyer. Miniature.

4 × 4cm

*Lent by the National Portrait Gallery*

As Commander-in-Chief of the British forces in North America Gage (1721–87) was well liked and respected by the Americans, with whom he had spent nearly twenty years of his army service. He arrived at Boston on 13 May 1774 with orders to transfer the seat of government to Salem and to implement the coercive Acts. By September he and his appointed council were isolated at Boston, protected by British troops from the rest of the hostile Bay province. With his mission an evident failure, he became anxious to resort to military action, as he explained to Lord Dartmouth in January 1775: 'If a respectable Force is seen in the Field, the most obnoxious of the Leaders seized, and a Pardon proclaimed for all others, that Government will come off victorious.'

The BOSTONIANS in DISTRESS.

19

### 19 Boston Blockaded, 1774

The Bostonians in Distress. (By Philip Dawe?)
London: Printed for R. Sayer, & J. Bennett,
1774

Mezzotint 35 × 26cm

*BM Department of Prints and Drawings, Satires* 5241

An English satire on the punishment meted out
to Boston for the Tea Party. Starving Bostonians imprisoned in a cage hung on their own
'Liberty Tree' are being fed fish by other colonists while British troops and cannon surround
them. In the bay four British warships lie at
anchor. Under the Boston Port Act of 1774
goods were to be landed at Marblehead near
Salem rather than Boston, and thence conveyed
overland to Boston. To relieve the Bostonians'
distress contributions of food and fuel were sent
from other towns, including 207 quintals of
codfish from Marblehead. In the summer of 1774
Gage ordered several infantry regiments supported by artillery to Boston Neck; an act which
was seen as an attempt to overawe the town.

### 20 Lord North and his Policy Ridiculed

'Boreas' (Lord North 1732–92)

An engraving from *The Oxford Magazine* Sept.
1774. Vol XI. p. 276.

13 × 21cm

*BM Department of Prints and Drawings, Satires* 5231

According to the writer and wit Horace Walpole,
Lord North had 'two prominent eyes that rolled
about to no purpose (for he was utterly short-
sighted), a wide mouth, thick lips and inflated
visage which gave him the air of a blind trum-
peter': features which made him easy prey for
cartoonists in time of political crisis. In 1774
with the coercive Acts against Massachusetts
Bay proceeding through Parliament the Whig
opposition took delight in ridiculing Lord North
and his policy.

20

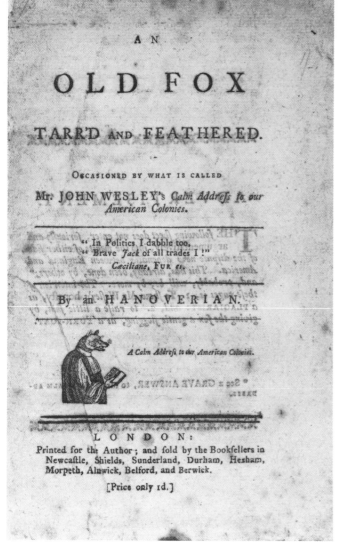

AN

# OLD FOX

### TARR'D AND FEATHERED.

OCCASIONED BY WHAT IS CALLED

Mr. JOHN WESLEY's *Calm Address to our American Colonies.*

" In Politics I dabble too,
" Brave *Jack* of all trades I !"
*Ceciliane*, FUR *et*.

By an HANOVERIAN.

*A Calm Address to our American Colonies.*

° See a GRAVE ANSWER, &c.

LONDON:

Printed for the Author; and fold by the Bookfellers in Newcaftle, Shields, Sunderland, Durham, Hexham, Morpeth, Alnwick, Belford, and Berwick.

[Price only 1d.]

23

## 21 A Friend to Liberty and Property, 1775

The Speech of the Right Hon. John Wilkes, Esq. Lord Mayor of the City of London, in the House of Commons on Wednesday, 8 February 1775 . . . on the American Taxation Bills.
London: Printed for E. Johnson, [1775].

*BL Department of Printed Books* 102.*h*.32

In 1774 Wilkes once more became the symbol of both British and American liberties as he fought to be re-elected to the House of Commons, despite his imprisonment in King's Bench prison in 1768. He was at last successful, taking his seat in the Commons unopposed on 2 December 1774. He lost no time in attacking Lord North's coercive policy towards America, and in his memorable speech of 8 February 1775 he questioned Parliament's assumed right of taxation 'the primary cause of the present Quarrel'. He argued that the 'Laws of Society are professedly calculated to secure the property of each Individual', and that North's policy would dismember 'the whole Continent [America] . . . from Great Britain, and *the wide Arch of the raised Empire fall*.'

## 22 Pamphlet Warfare, 1775

A calm address to our American Colonies. By John Wesley. London, Printed by R. Hawes [1775].

20cm

*BL Department of Printed Books* 8175.*a*.70

**23** An Old Fox Tarr'd and Feathered. Occasioned by what is called John Wesley's Calm Address to our American Colonies. By an Hanoverian [Augustus Montague Toplady].
London: Printed for the Author, 1775.

20cm

*BL Department of Printed Books* 8175.*b*.32

The approaching war in 1775 occasioned a number of loyalist pamphlets as well as those which flowed from radical pens. Typical of many was John Wesley's *Calm Address* which followed Samuel Johnson's argument in his *Taxation no Tyranny*, 1775. Wesley's longstanding doctrinal opponent, Augustus M. Toplady, author of the hymn 'Rock of Ages', took the opportunity to point out Wesley's plagiarism, as he termed it, by bracketing with malicious delight certain passages from Johnson's pamphlet with those of Wesley. Warning his countrymen against the designs of men who would 'overturn the English government', Wesley argued that the colonists had the same rights as their English-born ancestors but no more, and that they had, in return for their English privileges, 'ceded to the King and Parliament, *the power* of disposing without their consent, of both *their lives, liberties and properties*'. Toplady, mocking Wesley's conversion to a Tory view, quoted his earlier work *Thoughts on the Origin of Power*, 1772: 'No Man can dispose of another's life but by his own consent.'

The *Calm Address* was to be sold at the Foundry, Moorfields, a disused ordnance factory where Wesley had established his first headquarters for Methodism.

24

**24 A portrait of John Wesley (1703–91)**

John Wesley MA Fellow of Lincoln College Oxford. Done from an original in the possession of Thos Woolridge Esq. of East Florida. Nath! Hone Pinx! John Greenwood fecit. London, 1770.

*BM Department of Prints and Drawings,* 1877–8–11 –817

Westminster Mag. Dec. 1774.

Dec. 1774

*The Council of the*
*Rulers, & the Elders against the Tribe of ye Americanites.*

25

news of the First Continental Congress reached London in December, Lord North maintained what Thomas Hutchinson called, a 'strange silence upon American affairs' while he prepared to retaliate further against the colonies with a bill prohibiting the New England colonies from both trading and fishing.

This satire shows Lord North ('Boreas') in the House of Commons bribing supporters to vote 'unanimously and shamefully . . . against the peace and posterity of this new tribe [America]'. John Wilkes, robed as Lord Mayor of London, points an accusing finger and holds a 'Remonstrance against the Proceedings of the Min.r of the Prince'. In the background, as the members deliberate, a map of North America bursts into flames.

## *American reaction and attitudes 1764–75*

### 26 Boston, Massachusetts Bay Province

A South East view of ye Great Town of Boston in New England in America. W. Burgis delin. Printed & sold by W.m Price. Boston [c.1736].

60 × 131cm

*BL Map Library K. Top. CXX. 38a*

Boasting a population of 250,000 and a full treasury, Massachusetts Bay Province became the leader of American protest against British policy. Although challenged latterly by Philadelphia and New York, Boston remained the heart of a commercial empire extending from North Carolina to Nova Scotia. This view shows the town of Boston in the mid-eighteenth century. In the top left corner can just be seen the South-Meeting House (numbered 10) where Samuel Adams and his fellows met to discuss the Tea Act and past which the 'Indians' hastened to destroy the tea in Boston harbour on 16 December 1773 (see no. 37).

### 25 With Fire and Sword, 1775

The Council of the Rulers, & the Elders against the Tribe of ye Americanites. Engraved cartoon.

15 × 10cm

From *Westminster Magazine,* Vol II, 1774.

*BM Department of Prints and Drawings, Satires* 5281

On 18 November 1774 George III, writing to Lord North, acknowledged that 'the New England Governments are in a state of Rebellion, blows must decide whether they are to be subject to this Country or independent'. When

A South East View of y<sup>e</sup> Great Town of Boston in New England in America

26

I. DICKINSON ESQ.<sup>R</sup>  B.B.E.

*Member of Congrefs & Author of the Letters of a Farmer of Penfylvania.*

*Pub.<sup>d</sup> May 15.<sup>th</sup> 1783, by R. Wilkinson, N.<sup>o</sup> 58, Cornhill, London.*

29

## 27 No Taxation Without Representation

The Rights of the British Colonies asserted and proved. By James Otis, Esq. London: Reprinted for J. Almon [*c.*1772].

21cm

*BL Department of Printed Books* 102.*e*.10

The best known exponent of the American view of Parliament's power to legislate was the lawyer and publicist James Otis (1725–83), who with Samuel Adams led the radical party of opposition in the Massachusetts House of Representatives, until his increasingly frequent bouts of insanity forced him to retire in 1771. In his popular pamphlet *The Rights of the Colonies Asserted* Otis set distinct limits to the powers of Parliament to legislate for the colonies, drawing his argument mainly from the writings of Chief Justice Coke (1552–1634) and John Locke (1632–1724). 'If the reasons that can be given against an act', wrote Otis, 'are such as plainly demonstrate that it is against natural equity, the

executive courts will adjudge such acts void.' By contrast in England it was becoming accepted that an Act of Parliament must be upheld by the courts even if it were unconstitutional. Otis's view coupled with his reiteration of Locke's principle that 'no taxes shall be raised on the property of the people without the consent of the people given by themselves or their deputies' (which was manifestly not the American situation), provided the theoretical basis of opposition to the British Government. In Governor Barnard's words 'the Taxability and not the Tax is what pinches'.

## 28 Letters from a Farmer in Pennsylvania to the inhabitants of the British Colonies [By John Dickinson]. Philadelphia: Printed by David Hall and William Sellers, 1768.

20cm

*BL Department of Printed Books* 8175.*aa*.42

First published on 2 December 1767 in the *Pennsylvania Chronicle*, the *Letters* denied the authority of Parliament to levy taxes of any sort upon the colonies and advocated the non-importation of British manufactures. 'If you once admit that Great-Britain may lay duties upon her exportations to us, for the purpose of levying money on us only, she then will have nothing to do, but to lay those duties on the articles which she prohibits us to manufacture . . . and the tragedy of American liberty is finished.' John Dickinson did not approve of violent resistance to the Stamp Act and the later Townshend Revenue Acts, and he agreed with William Pitt that Parliament had the right to regulate colonial commerce and prohibit American manufacture. In spite of some of the conservative attitudes expressed in the *Letters* they became the political watchword of the Americans before the War.

## 29 John Dickinson (1732–1808)

I. Dickinson Esq. Member of Congress and Author of the Letters of a Farmer of Pennsylvania. London, 1783.

An engraved portrait.

27 × 23cm

*BM Department of Prints and Drawings*, 1862–12–13–88

Although both a lawyer and landowner, Dickinson spent much of his career until his eclipse by more radical contemporaries arguing opposition to Great Britain's new colonial policy. He was a delegate to the Stamp Act congress, to the First and Second Continental Congresses (1774, 1775), and drew up both the 'Declaration of the causes for taking up arms' and the later conciliatory Olive Branch petition in 1775. An advocate of compromise, he voted against the Declaration of Independence but fought in the War as a Patriot.

## 30 Rioting in Boston, 1770

The Fruits of Arbitrary power; or the Bloody Massacre, perpetrated in King-Street, Boston, by a party of the XXIXth Regt.

37 × 24cm

In *A Short Narrative of the Horrid Massacre in Boston* ... London: W. Bingley, 1770.

Inscribed: 'Presented by Thomas Hollis Esq., May 14, 1770'.

*BL Department of Printed Books* 1061. *h*.11

Typical of the many clashes in Boston and elsewhere which occurred after the enactment of Townshend's Act (see no. 12) was the notorious Boston massacre. On 5 March following a fight between rope-makers and a group of the garrisoned soldiers a mob marched on the Customs House which was protected by only one sentry. Reinforcements under the command of Captain Preston failed to quell the crowd and, apparently without Preston's command, the soldiers fired, killing three and fatally wounding two people. Writing to General Gage from Boston gaol on 19 March, Preston asserted that he 'went to the fatal place purely from that motive, to passefy the Mob if possible, to support the sentry in his material trust, & restrain the soldiers by my presence, from committing the mischiefs that

30

happened; but the mob were violent & the soldiers insulted & struck were stimulated to execute the tragical scene'. Defended by Robert Auchmuty, John Adams and Josiah Quincy Jr, Preston and all the defendants, except two convicted of manslaughter, were acquitted.

This engraving of the massacre seems to have been copied from the print made by the later loyalist Henry Pelham (1749–1806), who accused Paul Revere of plagiarism when he learnt Revere was 'cutting a plate of the late Murder'. Revere's print was published a full week before Pelham's and served as a major piece of propaganda for the radicals.

This copy was presented to the Library by that 'true Whig' and 'friend of liberty', Thomas Hollis (1720–74).

The Hon^ble JOHN HANCOCK.

*of BOSTON in NEW-ENGLAND, PRESIDENT of the AMERICAN CONGRESS.*
*Done from an Original Picture Painted by Littleford*

*London, Published as the Act directs 15 Octr 1775 by C. Shepherd*

31

### 31 John Hancock, Patriot

The Hon^ble John Hancock of Boston in New-England; President of the American Congress. Done from an Original Picture Painted by Littleford. London: Published by C. Shepherd, 1775.

30 × 26cm

*BM Department of Prints and Drawings,* 1927–10–8–304

The richest New Englander on the patriot side, John Hancock (1736–93), Boston merchant and politician, became the idol of the populace after the *Liberty* affair, 1768 (see no. 13). He was elected to the General Court, and made Head of the Town Committee, and in 1774 delivered the commemorative address on the Boston Massacre. As president of the Second Continental Congress he signed the Declaration of Independence in flamboyant style but resigned in 1777,

disgruntled by the appointment of George Washington as Commander-in-Chief. Returning to Massachusetts politics, he became the state's first governor in 1780.

### 32 Hancock's Address on the Boston Massacre, 1774

An Oration delivered 5 March 1774, at the request of the inhabitants of the town of Boston: to commemorate the Bloody Tragedy of the Fifth of March 1770. By the Honorable John Hancock, Esq. Boston: Edes and Gill, 1774.

20cm

*BL Department of Printed Books* 1324.c.5

On 8 April 1771 the Boston town meeting agreed 'to perpetuate the memory of that wanton and bloody massacre to all Generations' by establishing an oration each anniversary. In 1774, while Boston was under blockade, John Hancock roused his audience with a call to arms against the 'most formidable troops that ever trod the earth', recalling 'the inhuman, unprovoked murders of the fifth of March' and describing the town's present predicament: 'the town of Boston, ever faithful to the British Crown, has been invested by a British fleet: the Troops of George the Third have cross'd the wide atlantick, not to engage an enemy, but to assist a band of TRAITORS in Trampling on the rights and liberties of his most loyal subjects in America.'

### 33 Samuel Adams, revolutionary (1722–1803)

Samuel Adams Esq.

Engraved portrait.

18 × 11cm

*BM Department of Prints and Drawings,* 1913–4–15–124

Born into a Boston society family, Adams espoused the cause of opposition in preference to the family business which he nearly ruined. By 1763 he was a member of the influential Caucus club which met to drink 'flip' and smoke tobacco while planning the town's business before the assembly met. As Clerk to the Massachusetts House of Representatives, Adams led the radical party on Otis's retirement and promoted opposition to Governor Hutchinson, to Townshend's Acts, and to the garrisoning of troops in Boston, by writing vituperative pamphlets warning people of the conspiracy to take away their liberty and property. He advanced the radical idea that colonial assemblies were 'subordinate' but not 'subject' to Parliament and that they were obliged to guarantee the natural and constitutional rights of Americans even in the face of parliamentary legislation. Governor Hutchinson pronounced the Loyalist view of Adams when he remarked, 'I doubt whether there is a greater incendiary in the King's dominion or a man of greater malignity of heart'.

### 34 Liberty and Property, 1772

The Votes and Proceedings of the Freeholders and other Inhabitants of the Town of Boston. Boston: Printed by Edes and Gill, [1772].

20cm

*BL Department of Printed Books* 8175. *aa.*25

After 1770 relative calm prevailed in the Massachusetts Bay province but suspicion of the Government's intentions and an active will to resist any apparent encroachment on colonial liberties were translated into a number of co-operative ventures between towns and provinces, notably the Committee of Correspondence. In 1772 Adams set up a committee 'to state the rights of the Colonists and of this Province in particular, as men, as Christians, and as subjects; and to communicate the same to the several towns and to the world'. Having stated the colonists' natural rights to Life, Liberty and Property, the British Parliament's twelve violations were then listed in detail: '1st. The British Parliament have assumed the Powers of Legislation for the Colonists in all Cases whatsoever, without obtaining the Consent of the Inhabitants. . . . 2dly. They have exerted that assumed Power, in raising a Revenue in the Colonies

SAMUEL ADAMS Esq.
One of the DELEGATES *from the Province of* MASSACHUSETTS-BAY *to the General Continental* CONGRESS *of* NORTH-AMERICA.

33

without their consent; 3rdly. A Number of new Officers [the customs officers] . . . have been appointed to superintend this Revenue. . . . 9thly. The erecting of Slitting-Mills for manufacturing our iron . . . is an Infringement of that Right with which God and Nature have invested us . . . and we look upon the Restraint laid upon the Manufacture and Transportation of that to be . . . grievous . . .' The accompanying letter to the Towns stressed that this 'Plan of Despotism . . . is rapidly hastening to a completion . . . under a constant unremitted, uniform Aim to enslave us'.

35

### 35 Thomas Hutchinson, (1711–80) Governor of Massachusetts

Portrait by Edward Truman

Photograph of the original in the Massachusetts Historical Society

With his wealth, abilities, and family connections, Thomas Hutchinson played a large part in public life from his election to the House of Representatives in 1749 until his exile as Royal Governor from the province in 1774. He aroused the antagonism of both Samuel Adams and James Otis, by opposing the Land Bank established in 1740, in which Adams's father was a director, and by being appointed Chief Justice in 1760 instead of Otis's father. Although he disapproved of the British Government's various revenue-raising Acts as prejudicial to colonial trade, he never objected to Parliament's right to tax, and was firmly identified by the radicals as the leader of the Loyalist party. On 20 August 1765, the Boston mob destroyed his mansion in Garden Court Street and 'cast into the street, or carried away all his money, plate and furniture . . . his apparel, books, and papers'. He served as Governor from 1769 until the Tea Party incident made his position untenable. He continually complained to England that His Majesty's servants were not adequately supported and he insisted increasingly that the 'great thing now is to keep up the sense of our constitutional dependence, and an opinion that Parliament will maintain its supreme authority'.

### 36 American Liberties Threatened, 1773

Copy of letters sent to Great-Britain, by his Excellency Thomas Hutchinson, the Hon. Andrew Oliver, and several other Persons, born and educated among us. Boston: Edes and Gill, 1773.

19cm

*BL Department of Printed Books C.115.d.3*

In reply to Adams's *Rights of the Colonists*, 1772, Hutchinson presented before the General Court, on 6 January 1773, an elaborately argued address designed to prove that since 'no line can be drawn between the supreme authority of Parliament and the total independence of the colonies, Parliamentary supremacy must be admitted'. To retaliate, Adams and Hancock made much of thirteen letters obtained from Benjamin Franklin, which Hutchinson and others had sent to England. Ajudging 'that the Tendency and Design of the Letters . . . was to overthrow the Constitution of this Government, and to introduce arbitrary Power into the Province', the Boston printers, Edes and Gill, were instructed to print a sufficient number of copies of the letters for the perusal of the House which subsequently resolved to petition George III for Hutchinson's removal from office. Hutchinson maintained there was nothing in the letters which he had not stated publicly, but he must have preferred that his sentiments expressed in a letter of 20 January 1769 had remained undisclosed: 'I doubt whether it is possible to project a system of government, in which a colony 3,000 miles distant from the

Destruction of Tea in Boston Harbour. From B. J. Lossing, *1776*, 1849.

parent state shall enjoy all the liberty of the parent state. . . . I wish the good of the colony when I wish to see some further restraint of liberty rather than the connexion with the parent state should be broken; for I am sure such a breach must prove the ruin of the colony.'

## 37 The Boston Tea Party, 1773

Letter from Samuel Cooper of Boston to Benjamin Franklin dated 17 December 1773, describing colonial opposition to the recent Tea Act and the events culminating in the Boston Tea Party of 16 December.

MS, autograph

26 × 38cm

*BL Department of Manuscripts, King's MS 203.ff.* 15–16

On 18 November the *Dartmouth* anchored at the Long Wharf in Boston harbour with that 'worst of plagues, the detested tea', for distribution to East India Company consignees, Richard Clarke, Benjamin Faneuil, and to the governor's sons Thomas and Elisha Hutchinson. The owner of the ship, Francis Rotch, agreed under pressure

from a meeting of the townspeople convened by the Committee of Correspondence to return the tea to London without payment of the American duty. Unable to obtain clearance papers from the Customs House or a pass from the governor, the ship had still not sailed on 14 December. Preparations were then made by the Bostonians to dump the tea in the harbour. As Samuel Cooper described to Benjamin Franklin, 'two or three hundred Persons in Dress & appearance like Indians, passed by ye old South Meeting House, where the Assembly was held, gave a War Hoop, & hasten'd to the Wharf [Griffins Wharf] where all the Tea Ships lay, and demanding the Tea, which was given up to them without the least Resistance, they soon emptied all the Chests into the Harbor . . . . This was done without Injury to any other Property, or to any man's person; An interloper indeed, who had found means to fill his Pockets with Tea, upon being discovered was stript of his Booty, & his cloaths together, & sent home naked . . . .' Boston opposition to the Tea Act soon spread to the other colonies where similar mercantile interests were threatened by the East India Company. (see no. 16).

A New Method of MACARONY MAKING, as practiſed
217      at BOSTON in NORTH AMERICA.

*Printed for Carington Bowles, Nº 69 in Sᵗ Pauls Church Yard, London. Published 12 Octʳ 1774.*

38

## 38 The Fate of a Boston Customs Officer, 1774

A new method of macarony making, as practised at Boston in North America. London: Printed for Carington Bowles, 1774.

Mezzotint

14 × 11 cm

*BM Department of Prints and Drawings J5–67*

The hatred felt by Bostonians for British officials was well demonstrated in 1774, when John Malcom, a Customs officer, wounded a towns-man. Tarred and feathered, Malcom was chained to the Liberty tree, forced to drink quantities of tea, the symbol of British tyranny, and threatened with a hanging if he did not resign his commission. The cartoon shows Malcom being turned into a 'macarony' or fop American style. At his side stand two patriots; one sporting the favour of the militant organization the Sons of Liberty in his hat brim, the other bearing the number '45' on his hat; an allusion to John Wilkes's infamous paper the *North Briton* No. 45 (see no. 14).

## 39 The First Continental Congress, 1774

Petition of the Congress, held at Philadelphia,
5 September 1774.

53 × 38cm

*Lent by the Public Record Office, C.O.5/75 pt 2
pp 236–9*

On hearing that Boston had been blockaded in
May 1774 (see no. 19) the Virginian House of
Burgesses, led by Patrick Henry, recommended
that a congress of delegates from the thirteen
colonies be held to force a general redress of
grievances. The First Continental Congress met
from 5 September to 26 October in Philadelphia,
and resolved to support Massachusetts Bay by a
formal agreement not to import, or consume,
goods from Great Britain until the 'Intolerable
Acts' were repealed. Some delegates favoured
military preparations, but as John Adams remarked 'the delegates' opinions are fixed against
hostilities and ruptures except they should become absolutely necessary, and this necessity
they do not yet see'. Instead, they petitioned
George III for a return to the colonial situation
prevailing at the end of the Seven Years' War:
'From this destructive system of colony administration adopted since the conclusion of the last
war, have flowed those distresses dangers fears and
jealousies that overwhelm your majesty's dutiful
colonists with affliction. . . . We ask but for
peace, liberty and safety.'

## 40 Philadelphia

Second street North from Market St. w^th Christ
Church, Philadelphia. Drawn and engraved by
W. Birch & Son. Philadelphia: R. Campbell &
Co., 1799.

In: William Birch, *Views of Philadelphia* [1800]

40 × 49cm

*BL Map Library Maps C.7.e.14*

Charles Thomson, secretary of the Pennsylvania
Committee of Correspondence, on 18 June 1774

suggested the town of Philadelphia as a suitable
place for the First Continental Congress as few
regular British troops were stationed nearby. The
State House was not available to the delegates,
Governor Penn being mindful of his official position, and so Carpenters' Hall, set back from
Chesnut Street, was decided upon as a meeting
place for the First Continental Congress. The
*Royalist* newspaper warned the Company that
the Hall might be confiscated and 'their necks
inconveniently lengthened'.

## 41 A Loyalist Solution, 1774

A plan of a proposed union between Great-
Britain and the Colonies of New-Hampshire,
Massachusetts-Bay [etc.] which was produced by
one of the Delegates from Pennsylvania, in Congress . . . [By Joseph Galloway] London, 1775.

21cm

*BL Department of Printed Books 102.f.63*

On 28 September 1774 Joseph Galloway (*c.*1731–
1803), Loyalist lawyer and Pennsylvanian delegate to the First Continental Congress, rose to
deliver an address advocating a novel constitutional settlement between Great Britain and
America which would reorganize the Empire. A
central American government to be administered
by a President General appointed by the King,
with a Grand Council elected by the colonies,
was to determine 'all the general polity and
affairs of the colonies'. Laws for America, framed
in the House of Commons, were to be submitted
to the Grand Council for approval. The mood of
the Congress was not conciliatory. Patrick Henry
opposed Galloway's plan, asserting that the
colonies would be thrown 'into the Arms of an
American Legislature that may be bribed by that
Nation which avows . . . that Bribery is a Part of
her System of Government'. All reference to
Galloway's proposal was expunged from the
Congress minutes.

PATRICK HENRY
Nat-1736 – Ob-1799.

*From the Original Painting in the possession of the Family.*

42

**42 Patrick Henry, revolutionary orator (1736–99)**

Patrick Henry. Etched by Albert Rosenthal Phila. 1888. From the original painting in the possession of the family.

25 × 15cm

*BM Department of Prints and Drawings* 1936–12–7–43

Turning from a ruinous business career, Patrick Henry obtained a licence to practise law and in 1765 was elected to the Virginian House of Burgesses. He led opposition to Great Britain's colonial policy by his notable powers of oratory and his insistence that the Virginian legislature should be independent. He proposed the First Continental Congress in 1774, and in March 1775 delivered a memorable speech to the provincial convention at Richmond, advocating that the colony be immediately put into a position of defence and that a plan be prepared 'for the embodying, arming and disciplining such a number of men as may be sufficient for the Purpose'. He ended on a dramatic note: 'Give me liberty or give me death.'

**43 New England**

Bowles' Map of the Seat of War in New England, comprehending the provinces of Massachusetts Bay and New Hampshire; with the colonies of Connecticut and Rhode Island . . . London: Carington Bowles, 1776.

1:2,500,000 approx.

52 × 63cm

*BL Map Library*, 1.*TAB*.44.(14)

According to a contemporary historian, the traveller passing through the northern provinces of the American colonies would find that, 'In New England, where nature has been less bountiful in the productions of the earth, he will find a race of men, healthy, strong and vigorous; keen, penetrating, active, and enterprising, with a degree of dexterity and management in all the common affairs of life, which approaches to cunning and artifice'. Such were the thousands of merchants and farmers who managed to keep Gage hemmed in at Boston with the only British force on the continent. By the beginning of 1775, the British ministry had reached the conclusion that 'New England, the heart of the trouble, must be severed from the middle colonies, ruined by the annihilation of her trade and fisheries, and harried by Canadian and Indian raiders 'til she turned to the British Army for protection.'

# II The Outbreak of War in New England
## 1775–76

By the Spring of 1775 the Patriot militia in Massachusetts numbered, according to John Adams's reckoning, about 25,000, and while they were 'not exact soldiers', they were all 'used to arms'. Military momentum gathered impetus as the committee of safety instructed the committee of supplies to 'purchase all kinds of War like stores, sufficient for an Army of fifteen thousand men to take to the field'. Gage's ineffectiveness in controlling what Dartmouth referred to as the 'tumultuous rabble' was clearly discerned in London. The Colonial Secretary, in a 'secret missive' which reached Gage on 16 April, plainly rebuked the Governor for his mishandling of the situation and instructed him that force was to be used to restore Royal Authority throughout Massachusetts. This was the signal for war to begin. Gage dispatched hundreds of redcoats to Concord to seize the military supplies which had been collected there.

The fatal clash between troops and civilians at Lexington and Concord produced, as Franklin prophesied, a 'breach that can never afterwards be healed'. Thousands of militia gathered around Boston in late April, confining the British troops to the town. Patriot resentment increased with the arrival of three British generals, sent to reinforce Gage's command in May, and was further provoked by Gage's proclamation of martial law on 12 June. The informed anticipation by the Americans of Gage's belated decision to fortify Bunker Hill, opposite Boston, led to the first major battle, fully committing the colonies to war. Although the British won the engagement, the Patriots scarcely felt defeated. Legislation for a Continental Army had meanwhile been passed by the Second Continental Congress, sitting in Philadelphia, and troops commanded by Washington held Boston in the tight grip of an unrelenting siege.

Even at this time, the reluctance of many Americans, like John Dickinson, irretrievably to sever relations with the mother country was mirrored in contradictory statements, such as the 'Causes and Necessity of Taking up Arms' and the Olive Branch Petition, issued in the summer of 1775. The rejection of this petition by the King merely stiffened the Patriots' resolve towards independence. The unlucky Gage was relieved of his command and was replaced by General Sir William Howe, who was to be no more fortunate than Gage in establishing authority in New England. After an exceptionally hard winter in Boston, Howe found himself in early March 1776 in a situation similar to that which confronted Gage at Bunker Hill. General Washington had forestalled him in fortifying Dorchester Heights, which overlooked Boston to the south-east, thereby posing an immediate threat to the safety of the town. Howe's attempt to dislodge the Americans from their new position failed, bad weather preventing the redcoats from sailing to Dorchester Neck. His only solution was finally to abandon Boston, an unwelcome admission of defeat, and the British troops were evacuated on 17 March 1776.

## 44 General Gage

General Gage. Photograph of the original in the possession of the Rt Hon. Viscount Gage.

Succeeding Thomas Hutchinson as Governor of Massachusetts in 1774 (see no. 18) Gage was expected to meet with fewer difficulties in accomplishing the task of restoring royal law and order to the province. Governor Gage would have no trouble in securing troops from General Gage. After Lexington and Concord it was evident that 'the enthusiastic zeal with which these people have behaved must convince every reasonable man what a difficult and unpleasant task General Gage has before him'. Lord George Germain did not think him equal to that task. 'I must then lament', he wrote, 'that General Gage, with all his good qualities, finds himself in a situation of too great importance for his talents. The conduct of such a war requires more than common abilities, the distance from the seat of Government necessarily leaves much to the discretion and resources of the general, and I doubt whether Mr Gage will venture to take a step beyond the letter of his instructions.' The King was opposed to disgracing Gage for his alleged mishandling of the situation, but after the Battle of Bunker Hill the cabinet insisted on Gage's return to England. He was recalled for 'consultations' in October 1775.

## 45 Lexington, 19 April 1775

The Battle of Lexington, April 19th 1775. Plate I. A. Doolittle. Sculpt. Photograph of the original in the Connecticut Historical Society.

Regarded as the opening episode of the War, the 'Battle of Lexington' lasted only about fifteen or twenty minutes. About seventy of the local company of Minute-Men, forewarned by Paul Revere and William Dawes of the advance of British troops, had armed themselves and, on Captain John Parker's instructions, assembled on Lexington Green. Just before dawn they were confronted by the advance party of six companies of regulars under the command of Major Pitcairn, who ordered the 'rebels' to disperse. Both sides persistently denied responsibility for the first shot to be fired. Captain Parker is said to have ordered, 'Don't fire unless fired upon. But if they want a war let it begin here.' Pitcairn wrote to Gage afterwards, 'I gave directions to the troops to move forward, but on no account to Fire, or even attempt it without orders.' The ill-trained militia retreated haphazardly, then, in the words of Paul Revere, the Boston silversmith, 'I saw, and heard, a gun fired . . . . Then I could distinguish two guns, and then a continual roar of musketry.' When order was finally restored the casualties numbered eight American dead and ten wounded; on the British side one soldier was wounded and Major Pitcairn's horse was grazed.

## 46 Concord, 19 April 1775

Bloody Butchery, by the British Troops, or The Runaway Fight of the Regulars. Being the Particulars of the Victorious Battle fought at and near Concord . . . [Salem, 1775].

51 × 40cm

*BL Department of Printed Books* 1851.c.10.(96)

Arriving at Concord the regulars discovered most of the military stores to have been removed or hidden. Burning and destroying what could be found, the main body of soldiers remained in the town, while some 300 light-infantrymen were sent to secure the North Bridge. Alarmed by the appearance of numbers of Minute-Men, these soldiers opened fire. Deadly retaliation by the provincials drove the regulars back to the main party, and as more militia assembled Col. Smith ordered a retreat. Gage's earlier assessment of the Americans, 'They will undoubtedly be lyons whilst we are lambs, but if we take the resolute part they will undoubtedly prove very meek', had been proved disastrously wrong. The American dead were memorialized in this Broadside, printed at the request of the friends of the

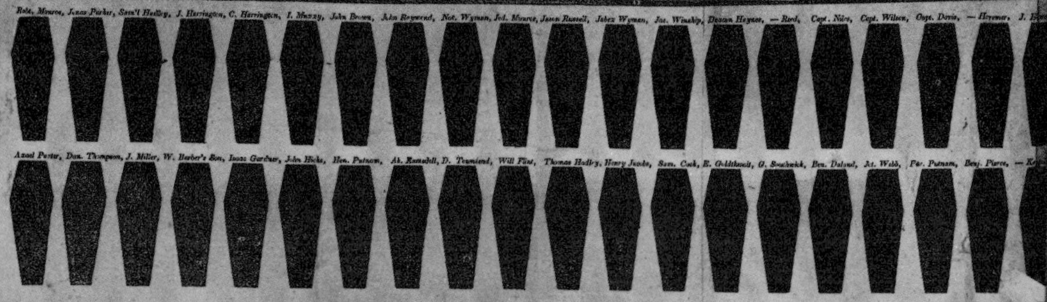
Robt. Monroe, Jonas Parker, Sam'l Hadley, J. Harrington, C. Harrington, I. Muzzy, John Brown, John Raymond, Nat. Wyman, Jed. Munroe, Jason Russell, Jabez Wyman, Jas. Winship, Deacon Haynes, — Reed, Capt. Niles, Capt. Wilson, Capt. Davis, — Hosmer, J.
Asael Porter, Dan. Thompson, J. Miller, W. Barber's Son, Isaac Gardner, John Hicks, Hen. Putnam, Ab. Ramsdell, D. Townsend, Will Flint, Thomas Hadley, Henry Jacobs, Sam. Cook, E. Goldthwait, G. Southwick, Ben. Daland, Jot. Webb, Per. Putnam, Benj. Pierce, — K

# BLOODY BUTCHERY,

BY THE

# BRITISH TROOPS;

OR THE

## RUNAWAY FIGHT OF THE REGULARS.

Being the **PARTICULARS** of the **VICTORIOUS BATTLE** fought at and near **CONCORD**, situated Twenty Miles from Boston, in the Province of the Ma-sachusetts-Bay, between Two Thousand Regular Troops, belonging to His Britannic Majesty, and a few Hundred Provincial Troops, belonging to the Province Massachusetts-Bay, which lasted from sunrise until sunset, on the 19th of April, 1775, when it was decided greatly in favor of the latter. These particulars published in this cheap form, at the request of the friends of the deceased **WORTHIES**, who died gloriously fighting in the CAUSE OF LIBERTY and their COUNT and it is their sincere desire that every Householder in the country, who are sincere well-wishers to America, may be possessed of the same, either to fra and glass, or otherwise to preserve in their houses, not only as a Token of Gratitude to the memory of the Deceased Forty Persons, but as a perpetual m morial of that important event, on which, perhaps, may depend the future Freedom and Greatness of the Commonwealth of America. To which is annexe Funeral Elegy on those who were slain in the Battle.

From E. RUSSELL'S *Salem Gazette*, or *Newbury* and *Marblehead Advertiser*, published on Friday, April 21, 1775.

ON Tuesday evening the eighteenth instant, a body of soldiers under the command of Lieutenant-Colonel *Smith*, to the amount of about eight hundred men, embarked from *Barton's Point* in *Boston*, about eleven o'clock, crossed *Charles-River*, landed at *Phips's-Farm*, in *Cambridge*, and marched immediately up to *Lexington*, near twelve miles from *Boston*; at sunrise they observing between thirty and forty inhabitants exercising near the meeting-house, the Commanding-Officer ordered them to lay down their arms and disperse, which not being directly complied with, he "*demanded them for a pack of rebels*," ordered his men to fire upon them, and killed eight men upon the spot, besides wounding several more. The army then proceeded to *Concord*, drew up on the parade, near the meeting-house, during which time the inhabitants from the neighboring towns collected and took possession of the adjacent hills; about eleven o'clock the firing began on both sides, which lasted near an hour, when the regular troops began to retreat, the provincials closely pursuing them to a bridge at a small distance, which the regulars took up as they passed; they then renewed the fire, and some were slain on both sides; but the regulars still retreated, and the provincials pursued them down to *Lexington*, where the regulars, about three o'clock in the afternoon, met with a reinforcement of about twelve hundred men commanded by Earl *Percy*, with two brass field pieces; they again renewed the attack upon the provincials, but soon thought proper further to retreat towards their head-quarters, the provincials pursued them into *Charlestown*, where they arrived at 6 o'clock; taking immediately, an advantageous post on *Bunker's-Hill*, about a mile from the ferry; the provincials now discontinued the pursuit. The loss on either side we have not yet been able to ascertain, but it is said about one hundred regulars were killed and fifty wounded, among which were several officers: Two officers and a number of soldiers were taken prisoners. On the part of the province, we hear that thirty-five were slain, and several wounded. The above is as particular an account of the engagement, as can at this time be collected, in the present confused state of the province.

We hear an officer and his servant, with two pair of pistols, were yesterday taken and secured by our people, at *Roxbury*, on their way to Castle-*William*.

S A L E M, April 25.

LAST Wednesday, the nineteenth of April, the troops of his *Britannic* Majesty commenced hostilities upon the people of this province, attended with circumstances of cruelty not less brutal than what our venerable Ancestors received from the vilest savages of the wilderness. The particulars relative to this interesting event, by which we are involved in all the horrors of a civil war, we have endeavored to collect as well as the present confused state of affairs will admit.

On Thursday evening a detachment from the army, consisting, it is said, of eight or nine hundred men, commanded by Lieutenant-Colonel *Smith*, embarked at the bottom of the common in *Boston*, on board a number of boats, and landed at *Philips's-farm*, [illegible] way up *Charles-River*, from whence they proceeded with silence and ex[illegible]on, on their way to *Concord*, about twenty miles from *Boston*. The people were soon alarmed, and began to assemble, in several towns, before day-light, in order to watch the motion of the troops. At *Lexington*, six miles below *Concord*, a company of militia, of about one hundred men, mustered near the meeting-house; the troops came in sight of them just before sunrise; and running within a few rods of them, the Commanding-Officer accosted the militia in words to this effect:—"*Disperse you rebels—Damn you throw down your arms and disperse;*" Upon which the troops huzza'd, and immediately one or two officers discharged their pistols, which were instantaneously followed by the firing of four or five of the soldiers, and then there seemed to be a general discharge from the whole body. Eight of our men were killed, and nine wounded. In a few minutes after this action the enemy renewed their march for *Concord*; at which place they destroyed several carriages, carriage-wheels, and about twenty barrels of flour, all belonging to the province. Here about one hundred men, going towards a bridge, of which the enemy were in possession, the latter fired, and killed two of our men, who then returned the fire, and obliged the enemy to retreat back to *Lexington*, where they met Lord *Percy*, with a large reinforcement, with two pieces of cannon. The enemy now having a body of about eighteen hundred men made a halt, picked up many of their dead, and took care of their wounded. At *Menotomy*, a few of the men, belonging to the detachment from *Lynn-End*, attacked a party of twelve of the enemy (carrying stores and provisions to the troops) killed two of them, wounded several, took six prisoners, shot five horses, and took possession of all their arms, stores, provisions, &c., without any loss on our side; among those who were killed was a Lieutenant, who went with the provisions for his recreation, and to view the country, the officer of the guard who generally attends on such occasions being only a serjant.—The enemy having halted one or two hours at *Lexington*, found it necessary to make a second retreat, carrying with them many of their dead and wounded, who they put into chaises and on horses that they found standing in the road. They continued their retreat from *Lexington* to *Charlestown* with great precipitation; and notwithstanding their field pieces, our people continued the pursuit, firing at them until they got to *Charlestown* neck, (which they reached a little after sunset) over which the enemy passed, proceeded up *Bunker's-Hill*, and soon afterwards went into the town, under the protection of the *Somerset* man of war of seventy-four guns.

In *Lexington* the enemy set fire to Deacon *Joseph's Loring's* house and barn, Mrs. *Mulliken's* house and shop, and Mr. *Joshua Bond's* house and shop, which were all consumed. The also set fire to several other houses, but our people extinguished the flames. They pillaged almost every house they passed by, breaking and destroying doors, windows, glasses, &c., and carrying off clothing and other valuable effects. It appeared to be their design to burn and destroy all before them; and nothing but our vigorous pursuit prevented their infernal purposes from being put in execution. But the savage barbarity exercised upon the bodies of our unfortunate brethren who fell, is almost incredible. Not content with shooting down the unarmed, aged, and infirm, they disregarded the cries of the wounded, killed them without mercy, and mangling their bodies in the most shocking manner.

We have the pleasure to say, that notwithstanding the highest provocations given by the enemy, not one instance of cruelty, that we have heard of was committed by our victorious militia; but, listened to the merciful dictates of the christian religion, they "breathed higher sentiments of humanity."

By an account of the loss of the enemy, said to have come from an officer of one of the men of war, it appears that sixty-three of the regulars, and forty-nine marines were killed, and one hundred and three of both wounded: In all two hundred and fifteen. Lieut. *Gould*, of the fourth regiment who is wounded, and Lieut. *Potter*, of the marines, and about twelve soldiers, are prisoners.

Mr. *James Howard* and one of the regulars discharged their pieces at the same instant, and each killed the other.

The public most sincerely sympathise with the friends, and relations of our deceased brethren, who gloriously sacrificed their lives in fighting for the liberties of their country. By their noble, intrepid conduct, in helping to defeat the forces of an ungrateful Tyrant, they have endeared their memories to the present generation, who will transmit their virtues down to the latest posterity.

The above account is the best we have been able to obtain. We can only add, that the town of *Boston* is now invested by a vast army of our brave countrymen, who have flown to our assistance from all quarters. GOD grant them assistance in the extirpation of our cruel and unnatural enemies.

S A L E M, May 5.

ON the nineteenth of April, was killed among others, by the *British* troops, at *Menotomy*, as he was courageously defending his country's rights, the good, the pious, and friendly Mr. DANIEL TOWNSEND, of *Lynn-End*. He was a constant and ready friend to the poor and afflicted; a good adviser in case of difficulty, and an able, mild, and sincere reprover of those who were out of the way. In short, he was a friend to his country, a blessing to society, and an ornament to the church of which he was a member. He has left an amiable consort, and five young children, to bewail the loss.

*Lie, valiant Townsend, in the peaceful shades.—We trust*
Immortal honors mingle with thy dust.
What! tho' thy body struggled in the gore;
So did thy Savior's body long before!
And as he rais'd his own, by power divine;
So the same power shall also quicken thine,
And in eternal glory mayst thou shine.

On Thursday the twentieth past, the bodies of eleven of the unfortunate persons who fell in the battle, were collected together and buried at *Medford*.

And on Friday the bodies of Messrs. Henry Jacobs, Samuel Cook, Ebenezer Goldthwait, George Southwick, Benjamin Daland, Jun. Jotham Webb, and Perley Putnam, of *Danvers*, who were likewise slain fighting in the GLORIOUS CAUSE OF LIBERTY AND THEIR COUNTRY, on the nineteenth of April, were respectfully interred among their friends in the different parishes belonging to that town, their corpse being attended to the place of interment by two companies of minute-men from this place, and a large concourse of people from this and the neighboring towns; previous to that interment, an excellent and well adapted prayer was delivered by the Rev. Mr. Holt, of that place.

Same day, the remains of Messrs. Asel Porter and Daniel Thompson, of *Woburn*, who also fell victims to tyranny, were decently interred at that place, attended to the grave by a multitude of persons who assembled on the occasion from that and the neighboring towns: Before they were interred, a very suitable sermon and prayer was delivered by the Rev. Mr. Sherman.

Captain Thomas Knights, of the fifth regiment, died at Boston the next day after the engagement, of his wounds he received in the same. He was greatly regretted being esteemed one of the best officers among the King's troops.

Lieut. Hull, of the regulars, died of his wounds on Wednesday last at the provincial hospital: His remains were next day conveyed to Charlestown, attended by a company of provincials, and several officers of distinction, and there delivered to the order of General Gage. Twenty-three wounded soldiers lately died at the Castle.

Lieutenant Hawkshaw was wounded in the cheek, and it is tho't will not recover.

Lieutenant Gore was wounded in the arm: About 12 other officers are wounded.

We can assure the public, from the best authority, that our brethren, of all the colonies which we can yet have heard from, are firm and unshaken in their attachment to the common cause of *America*; and that they are now ready, with their lives and fortunes, to assist us in defeating the cruel designs of our implacable enemies.

We have received no particulars of the transactions between General Gage and the inhabitants of *Boston*. It is certain that the people have delivered up their arms; very few of them have, however been permitted to leave the town, notwithstanding the promise of the General.

The following is a list of the Provincials who were KILLED and WOUNDED.

Belonging to *L E X I N G T O N.*

K I L L E D.

1 * Mr. Robert Monroe,
2 * Mr. Jonas Parker,
3 * Mr. Samuel Hadley,
4 * Mr. Jonathan Harrington,
5 * Mr. Caleb Harrington,
6 * Mr. Isaac Muzzy,
7 * Mr. John Brown,
8 Mr. John Raymond,
9 Mr. Nathaniel Wyman,
10 Mr. Jedediah Munroe.

W O U N D E D.

1 Mr. John Robbins
2 Mr. John Tidd
3 Mr. Solomon Pierce
4 Mr. Thomas Winship
5 Mr. Nathan Farmer
6 Mr. Joseph Amee
7 Mr. Ebenezer Munroe
8 Mr. Francis Brown
9 Prince Easterbrooks (a Negro Man)

*M E N O T O M Y.*

K I L L E D

11 Mr. Jason Russell
12 Mr. Jabez Wyman
13 Jason Winship

M I S S I N G, (supposed to be on board one of the men of war)

Mr. Samuel Frost
Mr. Seth Russell

*S U D B U R Y.*

K I L L E D

14 Deacon Haynes
15 Mr. —— Reed

*C O N C O R D.*

K I L L E D

16 Captain Miles

*B E D F O R D.*

K I L L E D

17 Captain Jonathan Willson

*A C T O N.*

K I L L E D

18 Captain Davis
19 Mr. —— Hosmer
20 Mr. James Howard

*W O B U R N.*

K I L L E D

21 * Mr. Asel Porter
22 Mr. Daniel Thompson

W O U N D E D

10 Mr. George Reed
11 Mr. Jacob Bacon

*C H A R L E S T O W N.*

K I L L E D

23 Mr. James Miller.
24 Captain William Barber's Son, aged

*B R O O K L I N E.*

K I L L E D

25 Isaac Gardiner, Esquire

*C A M B R I D G E.*

K I L L E D

26 Mr. John Hicks

*M E D F O R D.*

K I L L E D

27 Mr. Henry Putnam.

W O U N D E D

12 Mr. William Polly.

*L Y N N.*

K I L L E D

28 Mr. Abednego Ramsdell
29 Daniel Townsend
30 William Flint
31 Thomas Hadley

W O U N D E D

13 Mr. Joshua Felt
14 Mr. Timothy Munroe

*D A N V E R S.*

K I L L E D

32 Mr. Henry Jacobs
33 Mr. Samuel Cook
34 Mr. Ebenezer Goldthwait
35 Mr. George Southwick
36 Mr. Benjamin Daland, jun.
37 Mr. Jotham Webb
38 Perley Putnam

W O U N D E D

15 Mr. Nathan Putnam
16 Mr. Dennis Wallis

*S A L E M.*

K I L L E D

39 Mr. Benjamin Pierce

*B E V E R L Y.*

K I L L E D

40 —— Kennison

W O U N D E D

17 Mr. Samuel Woodbury
18 Mr. Nathaniel Cleaves

*F R A M I N G H A M.*

19 Mr. —— Hemmenway.

*B E D F O R D.*

20 Mr. John Lane.

*Those distinguished with this mark [*] were killed by the first fire of the enem*

A F U N E R A L

# ELEGY,

TO THE

IMMORTAL MEMORY

*Of those* WORTHIES *who were slain in the Battle of* CONCORD, *April* 19, 1775.

AID me ye nine! my muse assist,
A sad tale to relate,
When such a number of brave men
Met their unhappy fate.
At *Lexington* they met their foe
Completely all equipp'd,
Their guns & swords made glit'ring show,
But their base schemes were nipp'd.

*Americans*, go drop a tear
Where your slain brethren lay!
O! mourn and sympathize for them!
O! weep this very day!
What shall we say to this loud call
From the Almighty sent?
It surely bids both great and small
Seek GOD's face and repent.
Words can't express the ghastly scene
That here presents to view,
When forty of our brave countrymen
Sure bid their friends adieu.
O! think how awful it must seem,
To hear widows relent
Their husbands and their children
Who to their graves were sent.

The tender babes, nay those unborn,
O! dismal cruel death!
To snatch their fondest parents dear
And leave them thus bereft.
O! *Lexington*! your loss is great!
Alas! too great to tell;
But justice bids me to relate
What to you has befell.
Ten of your hardy, bravest sons,
Some in their prime did fall;
May we no more hear noise of guns,
To terrify us all.
Let's not forget the *Danvers* race,
So late in battle slain,
Their valor and their courage shown,
Upon this crimson'd plain.

Seven of your youthful sprightly sons
In the fierce fight were slain,
O! may your loss be all made up,
And prove a lasting gain.
*Cambridge* and *Medford's* loss is great,
Though not like *Acton's* town,
Where three fierce military sons
Met their untimely doom.
*Menotomy* and *Charlestown* met
A sore and heavy stroke,
In losing five of their townsmen
Who fell by a tyrant's yoke.
Unhappy *Lynn* and *Beverly*,
Your loss I do bemoan,
Five your brave sons in dust doth lie,
Who late were in the bloom.

*Bedford*, *Woburn*, *Sudbury*, all,
Have suffer'd most severe,
You miss five of your choicest chore,
On them let's drop a tear.
*Concord*, your Captain's fate rehearse,
His loss is felt severe,
Come, brethren, join with me in verse,
His mem'ry hence revere.
O! 'Squire *Gardiner's* death we feel,
And sympathizing mourn,
Let's drop a tear when it we tell,
And view his hapless urn.
We sore regret poor *Pierce's* death,
A stroke to *Salem* known,
Where tears did flow from every brow,
When the sad tidings come.

The groans of wounded, dying men
Would melt the stoutest soul,
O! how it strikes thro' every vein,
My flesh and blood runs cold.
May all prepare to meet their fate
At GOD's tribunal bar,
And may war's terrible alarm,
For death us now prepare.
Your country calls you far and near
*America's* sons awake,
Your helmet, buckler, and your spear
The LORD's own arm now make.
His shield will keep us from all harm
Tho' thousands 'gainst us rise,
His buckler we must sure put on,
If we would win the prize.

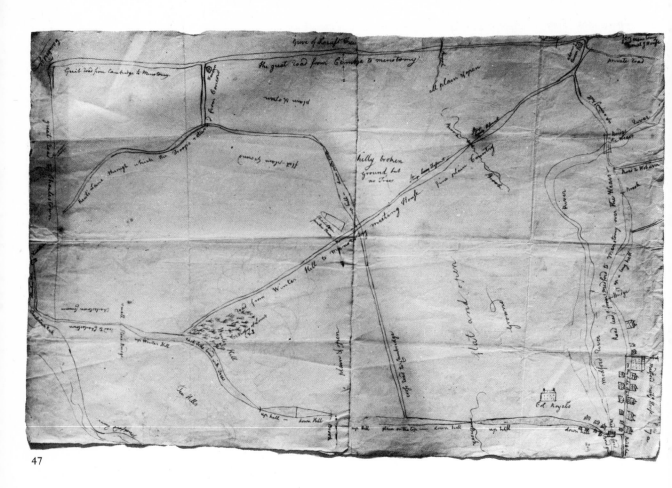

47

'deceased worthies . . . either to frame and glass, or otherwise to preserve'. British losses here and during the subsequent retreat were heavy; Germain 'had no conception the loss of troops could have been so great'.

### 47 Lord Percy's Return Route from Concord

[Sketch map of the roads between Cambridge, Menotomy, Charlestown and Medford. 1775.]
MS.
39 × 59cm
*Lent by His Grace the Duke of Northumberland*

This crude pen and ink road map appears to be the only document portraying Kent's Lane, the route by which Lord Percy returned from Concord to Charlestown, avoiding the patriot militia massed in Cambridge. The map depicts the 'great road from Cambridge to Menotomy' and the 'great road to Charlestown', among others. The gradient of the roads is given: 'up Hill – plain on the top – down hill', and the landscape is sketched in descriptive phrases: 'hilly broken ground but no trees', 'flat and open ground'.

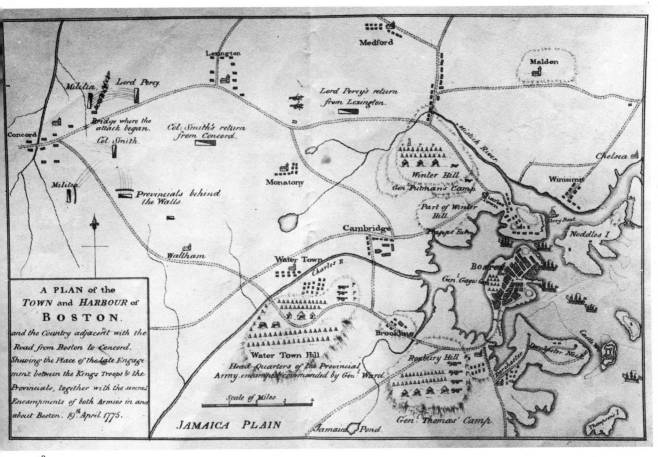

A PLAN of the
TOWN and HARBOUR of
BOSTON.
and the Country adjacent with the
Road from Boston to Concord.
Shewing the Place of the late Engage-
ment between the Kings Troops & the
Provincials, together with the several
Encampments of both Armies in and
about Boston. 19ᵗʰ April 1775.

48

## 48 The Retreat of the Regulars

A Plan of the Town and Harbour of Boston and the Country adjacent with the road from Boston to Concord. Showing the Place of the late Engagement between the King's Troops and the Provincials, together with the several Encampments of both Armies in and about Boston, 19 April, 1775.

MS, unsigned 1:126,720.

30 × 20cm

*Lent by His Grace the Duke of Northumberland*

The first known British map to show the retreat of the British troops from Concord on 19 April, this plan indicates the bridge at Concord where the militia opened fire on the regulars. Some inaccuracies appear on the map. Lord Percy, for example, did not advance beyond Lexington and he returned to Charlestown via Menatony (Arlington). The two cannon, brought by Lord Percy, can be seen just outside Lexington, where he encountered the retreating Col. Smith. Following on the events of Lexington and Concord, the Provincial Army about 9,000 strong, gathered around Boston with amazing speed. The positions of the army shown here suggest that the map was made on about 26 April. Formerly belonging to Lord Percy, this map is unique. A copy appears to have been sent to England where it was probably used as the basis for the more elaborate map published with additional information of a later date by I. de Costa in London on 29 July 1775.

### 49 Town Plan of Boston

A Plan of the Town of Boston, with the Intrenchments, *&c.* of His Majesty's Forces in 1775. From the Observations of Lieut. Page of His Majesty's Corps of Engineers; and from the plans of other Gentlemen. [London,] Engraved and printed for Wm. Faden, 1st Oct. 1777.

1:9,800 approx.

45 × 31cm

*BL Map Library* 73431.(1)

The most detailed plan of Boston for the period, this map shows troop locations, batteries, the fortifications on Boston Neck and the head-quarters of general officers. Some troop units are identified and the streets and principal places are named, giving a comprehensive picture of Boston in its last year under British authority. Under the supervision of Montresor, Gage's engineer, the old fortifications on Boston Neck were strengthened and added to in September 1774, a deep ditch was dug into which the tide flowed at high water, turning Boston into an island. By 20 April 1775, just after the battles of Lexington and Concord, Boston was besieged by provincial troops while a formidable military force was assembling within the town. Tents covered its fields, cannon were placed on the hills and troops paraded daily in the streets. It was a welcome sight only to the adherents of the British Ministry, for it was the one place in Massachusetts where the governor was in authority and where the laws of Parliament were still in force. Watching the growth of the rebellion and the gathering of the American army around Boston, Gage wrote: 'This province began it, I might say this Town, for here the Arch-Rebels formed their scheme long ago. This Circumstance brought the Troops first here which is the most disadvantageous Place for all Operations particularly where there is no Division of the Rebels' Forces, but all is collected into one Point.'

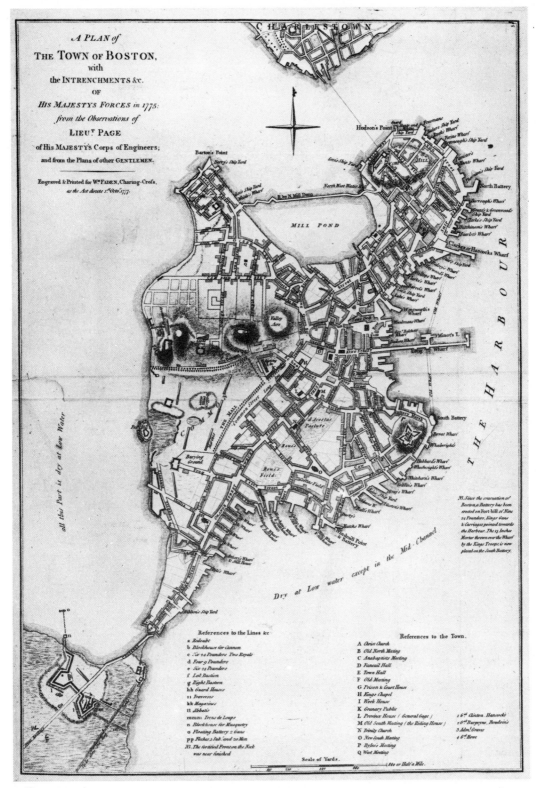

A PLAN of
THE TOWN of BOSTON,
with
the INTRENCHMENTS &c.
OF
HIS MAJESTYS FORCES in 1775:
from the Observations of
LIEUT PAGE
of His Majesty's Corps of Engineers;
and from the Plans of other GENTLEMEN.

Engraved & Printed for Wm FADEN, Charing-Cross,
as the Act directs 1st Octr 1777.

CHARLESTOWN

MILL POND

THE HARBOUR

**References to the Lines &c**
a Redoubt
b Blockhouse for Cannon
c Six 24 Pounders Two Royals
d Four 9 Pounders
e Six 24 Pounders
f Left Bastion
g Right Bastion
hh Guard Houses
ii Traverses
kk Magazines
ll Abbatis
mmm Trous de Loups
n Blockhouse for Musquetry
o Floating Battery 2 Guns
pp Fleches 1 Sub. and 20 Men
N1. The fortified Front on the Neck
was near finished

**References to the Town.**
A Christ Church
B Old North Meeting
C Anabaptists Meeting
D Faneuil Hall
E Town Hall
F Old Meeting
G Prison & Court House
H Kings Chapel
I Work House
K Granary Public
L Province House (General Gage)
M Old South Meeting (the Riding House)
N Trinity Church
O New South Meeting
P Byles's Meeting
Q West Meeting

1 Genl. Clinton. Hancock's
2 Genl. Burgoyne. Bowdoin's
3 Adml. Graves
4 Genl. Howe

Scale of Yards.

49

### 50 Gage's Proclamation, 12 June 1775

By his Excellency, The Hon. Thomas Gage Esq.,
Governor, and Commander in Chief, in and over
his Majesty's Province of Massachusetts-Bay,
and Vice-Admiral of the same. A Proclamation.
In: *The Remembrancer, or Impartial Repository of
Public Events,* Fourth edition, London, Printed
for J. Almon, 1775.

24cm

*BL Department of Printed Books PP.3435.ab*

On 5 May the Provincial Congress of Massachusetts Bay resolved that as General Gage had
'utterly disqualified himself to serve this colony
as Governor . . . he ought to be considered and
guarded against as an unnatural and inveterate
enemy to this country'. Against this background
of open opposition to the King, Gage wrote to
Dartmouth on 12 June; 'I see no prospect of any
offers of Accommodation and have issued a
Proclamation for the Exercise of the Law
Martial.' His proclamation, considered arrogant
and insulting by the colonists, addressed them as
'infatuated multitudes'. He pronounced those in
arms to be traitors but offered them the King's
pardon if they surrendered their weapons, 'excepting only from the benefit of such pardon
Samual Adams and John Hancock, whose
offences are of too flagitious a nature to admit of
any other consequence but condign punishment'.
Mrs Adams, in a letter to her husband John
Adams, dated 12 June 1775, expressed the common sentiment when she wrote; 'Gage's proclamation you will receive by this conveyance.
All the records of time cannot produce a blacker
page. Satan when driven from the regions of
bliss, exhibited not more malice. Surely the
father of lies is superseded.'

# The Battle of Bunker Hill, 17 June 1775

On 25 May the man-of-war *Cerberus* sailed into Boston Harbour with three major-generals, 'a triumvirate of reputation', on board. Sir William Howe, Sir Henry Clinton and John Burgoyne, with ministerial backing, had arrived to demand action. Informed that Boston was surrounded by 10,000 Provincials, Burgoyne exclaimed: 'What! Ten thousand peasants keep five thousand King's troops shut up! Well, let *us* get in and we'll soon find elbow-room.' Having issued a proclamation declaring martial law on 12 June, Gage, agreeing to a limited offensive, decided to take the strategic points of the Dorchester and Charlestown Heights; but the initiative was seized instead by the Massachusetts Committee of Safety, who had learned of Gage's plan.

Eighteen thousand Americans now surrounded Boston. Of these, about 3,000 under Col. William Prescott were detailed to fortify Charlestown Heights on the night of 16 June. On the morning of Saturday 17 June, Boston was woken by the roar of HMS *Lively*'s guns, aimed at the solid earthen redoubt which had been thrown up on Breeds Hill, just below Bunker Hill. Gage called a council of war; Clinton advised cutting off American retreat by attacking the rear of the Charlestown peninsula, but Gage was determined on a frontal approach to Prescott's entrenchments. The attack, commanded by Howe, was postponed until high tide, 2 pm, when British troops were landed at Moulton's Point. Howe's first move was a flanking manoeuvre to the right in an attempt to break through a fence which extended from the redoubt to the northern shore of the peninsula, and then to swing round and attack Prescott's rear. His first two advances met with a devastating musket volley from the Americans which decimated the front lines. Meanwhile, as Howe regrouped his forces for a final assault on Breeds Hill, Charlestown had been set on fire by shells from Boston. With only enough ammunition for one more round, the Americans were finally overwhelmed by British bayonets. Dr Joseph Warren, President of the Provincal Congress, was killed in the redoubt as the Americans retreated to Bunker Hill. The retreat continued across Charlestown Neck, which, raked by fire from HMS *Glasgow*, *Symmetry*, and floating batteries, was the scene of the greatest American casualties of the battle.

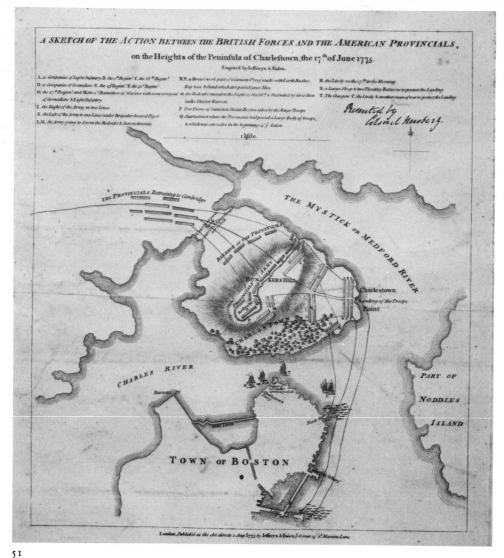

51

## 51 First Published Plan of the Battle of Bunker Hill

A Sketch of the Action Between the British Forces and the American Provincials, on the Heights of the Peninsula of Charlestown, the 17th June 1775. London, 1 August 1775, by Jefferys & Faden.

1:14,000 approx.

35 × 31cm

BL Map Library RUSI A30/3

The earliest published plan devoted wholly to the Battle of Bunker Hill, this map was printed only five days after news of the event reached London. Crude, and topographically inaccurate, this map does little to show the terrain which was ideal for American tactics: 'Fighting . . . among small enclosures and narrow lanes, they defended their position inch by inch.' After the battle, Gage wrote of the provincials: 'They showed a conduct and spirit against us, they never showed against the French, and everybody has judged them from their former appearance and behaviour'.

*Engraved for BARNARD's New Complete & Authentic HISTORY of ENGLAND.*

BOSTON

CHARLES TOWN

View of *The* ATTACK *on* BUNKER'S HILL, *with the* Burning *of* CHARLES TOWN, *June 17. 1775.*

*Drawn by Mr Millar.*                                                                                 *Engraved by Lodge.*

52

### 52 The Burning of Charlestown

View of the Attack on Bunker's Hill, with the Burning of Charlestown, June 17 1775. Drawn by Mr Millar. Engraved by Lodge. Engraved for Barnard's New Complete and Authentic History of England.

22 × 30cm

*BL Department of Printed Books Cup.* 1247.cc.17

Charlestown, the first settlement in the colony of Massachusetts Bay, was burned to the ground during the Battle of Bunker Hill. Believing its fate to be already sealed, as a result of constant threats of destruction by Gage should American troops remain there, most of the inhabitants had left Charlestown with their belongings. By 17 June not more than about 200 citizens remained of a population of two or three thousand. The order to set fire to Charlestown was finally given by Howe. The British forces moving to the attack on Breeds Hill were, according to Burgoyne, 'exceedingly hurt by musketry from Charlestown, though Clinton and I did not perceive it till Howe sent us word . . . and desired us to set fire to the town, which was immediately done; we threw a parcel of shells, and the whole was immediately in flames'. The buildings were mainly of wood, and the fire spread rapidly. Amos Farnsworth, a corporal in the Massachusetts militia, noted in his diary that the large and elegant buildings 'are almost laid in ashes by the barbarity and wanton cruelty of that infernal villain Thomas Gage'. The loss of property was estimated at £117,982 5s 2d, but applications for indemnification for these losses, made to Congress by the inhabitants, was refused.

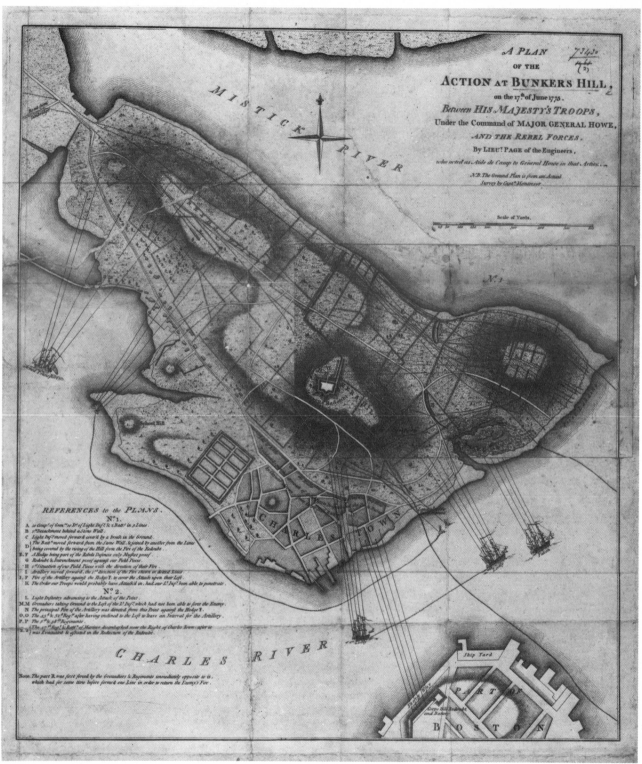

### 53 A Participant's Plan of Bunker Hill

A Plan of the Action at Bunkers Hill, on the 17th June 1775. Between His Majesty's Troops, under the command of Major General Howe, and the rebel forces. By Lieut. Page of the Engineers, who acted as Aide de Camp to General Howe in that Action. NB. The Ground Plan is from an Actual Survey by Capt. Montresor. [London: William Faden, between 1775 and 1778.]

1 : 4,900 approx.

49 × 43cm

*BL Map Library* 73430. (2)

Regarded as the most detailed delineation of the battle, this plan based on a survey by John Montresor, was drawn by another engineer, Lieut. Page. Both men were present at the battle, Page distinguishing himself in the storming of Warren's Redoubt, for which he received Howe's thanks. Seriously wounded in action, he was, according to the *London Chronicle* of 11 January 1776, 'the only one now living of those who acted as *Aide de Camp* to General Howe, so great was the slaughter of officers that day'.

The plan shows the lines of fire from the Corps Hill Battery in Boston and from the British ships on the Charles River. The initial attack by the British, which was repulsed, is shown on the overlay, while the successful offensive, which eventually penetrated the American defence, is given on the main map.

The Battle of Bunker Hill actually took place on Breeds Hill, but both are wrongly depicted on this plan, Breeds Hill having been substituted for Bunker Hill, whose greater elevation is mistakenly shown here in the south east of the peninsula instead of the north west. The error was not corrected in the subsequent reprinting of the map for Stedman's *History of the American War*, published in 1794.

### 54 Israel Putnam (1718–90)

Israel Putnam Esqr. Major General of the Connecticut Forces and Commander in Chief at the Engagement on Bunckers-Hill near Boston, 17 June 1775. London, Published ... by C. Shepherd, 9 September 1775.

36 × 24cm

*BM Department of Prints and Drawings, Satires* 5292

Veteran Indian fighter, Putnam was made Chairman of the local Committee of Correspondence by the town of Brooklyn in 1774. Visiting Boston in the same year, he stayed with Joseph Warren, and was made Lieut.-Colonel of the 11th Regiment of the Connecticut militia in 1775. Following the Battle of Bunker Hill, he was appointed major-general in the Continental Army.

Always convinced of the necessity of occupying Bunker Hill, Putnam accompanied Prescott's men when they fortified the lower Breeds Hill, but it was on Putnam's orders that smaller defence works were thrown up on Bunker Hill which would be of vital importance in covering a retreat. The six foot parapet and earth and wood firing platforms on Breeds Hill were apparently a response to Putnam's comment on the 'irregulars', that 'Americans were not afraid of their heads, though very much afraid of their legs; if you cover these they will fight forever'. Present at the fence when action began, he moved to Bunker Hill at the rear to urge on reinforcements, and it is to Putnam that the famous command, 'Men, you are all marksmen – don't one of you fire until you see the whites of their eyes', has been ascribed.

Contrary to some contemporary opinion, reflected in the title of this portrait, Putnam did not exercise any official authority or command in the battle. There seems to have been no authorized commander at Bunker Hill and Putnam served only as a volunteer.

55

## 55 Joseph Warren (1741–75)

Joseph Warren. Engraving

5 × 5cm

*BM Department of Prints and Drawings* 1867–3–9–1193

Born at Roxbury, Massachusetts, Warren established himself as a doctor in Boston, where he became friends with John Adams. Interesting himself in politics, he strongly supported the Whig cause, becoming a frequent contributor to the press. Head of the Boston delegation to the Provincial Congress in 1774, he was elected its President *pro tempore* in August the same year. An active member of most of the important local committees in 1775, and the only patriot leader to remain in Boston in the spring, it was he who, on 18 April, sent Paul Revere and William Dawes to Lexington to warn Adams and Hancock of their danger.

Elected a major-general by the Provincial Congress on 14 June, 'he did wonders in preserving order among the troops'. Warren joined the forces on Charlestown Heights on 17 June as a volunteer. Declining to take command, he

asked where he could be most useful, and directed to the redoubt by Putnam he replied: 'Don't think I come to seek a place of safety; but tell me where the onset will be most furious.' Putnam again pointed to the redoubt saying: 'That is the enemy's object, and if that can be defended the day is ours.'

One of the last to retreat, Warren was killed when the redoubt was finally taken by Howe's troops. His death at the age of thirty-four caused widespread despondency. John Adams's wife wrote; 'Not all the havoc and devastation they [the British] have made has wounded me like the death of Warren. We want him in the Senate; we want him in his profession; we want him in the field. We mourn for the citizen, the senator, the physician and the warrior.'

## 56 Gage's account of the Battle of Bunker Hill

Copy of a Letter from the Honourable Lieutenant General Gage to the Earl of Dartmouth. Dated Boston, 25 June 1775. In: *The London Gazette* numb. 11581. 22–25 July, 1775.

30cm

*BL Official Publications Library O.G.E.* 70

Gage's account of the Battle of Bunker Hill was received in London on 25 July 1775. In an accompanying letter to Dartmouth Gage wrote: 'The Success of which I send your Lordship an Account . . . was very Necessary in our Situation, and I wish most sincerely that it had not cost so dear. The number of the killed and wounded is greater than our Force can afford to lose.' British and American casualties were given in a wide range of conflicting statistics, but Gage reported 228 dead and 826 wounded of his troops while Washington reported the American losses at only 138 killed and 276 wounded. Explaining the disparity in numbers of casualties, which might appear to cede a numerical victory to the Provincials and reflect adversely on the British command, Gage noted that 'the Tryals we have had shew that the Rebels are not the despicable Rabble too many have supposed them to be'.

*Exposed to the Horrors of War, Pestilence and Famine, for a Farthing an Hour.*

*3 Shillings a Day. 2 Shillings a Day. 1 Shilling a Day.* SIX-PENCE A DAY. *Yankees. Fire and Water. Sword and Famine.*
*This Sketch displays the Hardships a Soldier and his Family endure on the bare Subsistance of Sixpence a Day, while the lowest Trades earn sufficient to enjoy the Comforts of Life.*

57

## 57 Winter in Boston

Six-pence a Day. Exposed to the Horrors of War, Pestilence and Famine for a Farthing an Hour. London, Publish'd 26 Octr. 1775 by W. Humphrey.

22 × 34cm

*BM Department of Prints and Drawings, Satires 5295*

Emphasizing the privations which a British soldier had to endure, this anti-recruiting satire contrasts his lot with that of the working man. In order to provide comforts for soldiers and to increase the bounty paid to recruits, subscriptions were raised locally. 'The situation of the troops,' wrote Lord Dartmouth on 5 September, 'cooped up in a town, exposed to insult and annoyance, if not to surprise, from more places than one, deprived of the comforts and necessaries of life, wasting away by disease and desertion faster than we can recruit, and no longer either the objects of terror or cause of distress to the rebels is truly alarming.' The situation deteriorated in December, by which time an unusually severe winter had set in. Food, clothing and fuel were scarce commodities in Boston, whereas the American army, although desperately short of fuel itself, was well supplied with food.

58

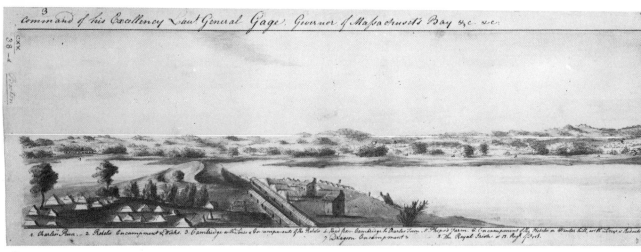

58

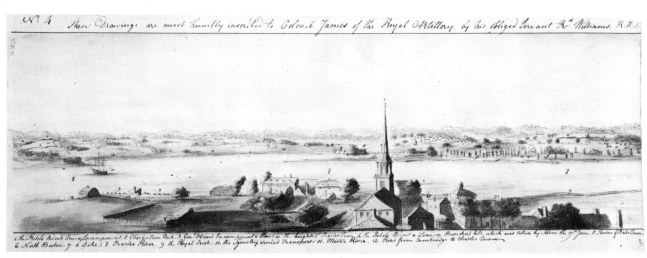

58

## 58 Boston Besieged

A view of the country round Boston, taken from Beacon Hill by Lieut. Williams of the Royal Welch Fuziliers, shewing the Lines, Redouts & Different Encampments of the Rebels allso those of his Majesty's Troops under the command of his Excellency Lieut. General Gage, Governor of Massachuset's Bay . . . 1775.

MS watercolour on paper. Each view 17 × 48cm

*BL Map Library K. Top. CXX. 38b–f*

This series of panoramic views, progressing from east to north, was drawn on Beacon Hill, situated on the western side of Boston. The regiment of Royal Welsh Fusiliers, to which the artist belonged, was posted at Fort Hill, on the eastern side of the town. During 1774 and 1775 these works housed about 400 men. Beginning with the view towards Castle Island to the east, the first drawing shows Dorchester Neck, which was to be fortified by Washington early in 1776, and part of Boston Common, where the British Marines and Artillery were encamped. The narrow isthmus of Boston Neck with the British lines is shown on the second view, together with John Hancock's house. On 22 December 1775 Congress passed a resolution authorizing Washington to make an assault on the British troops in Boston, 'notwithstanding the town, and property in it, might be destroyed'. Washington's headquarters were at Cambridge, seen in the third drawing while the following view shows the Charlestown promontory, the ruins of the town, burned down on the 17 June and General Howe's encampment which was set up on Bunker Hill after the Battle. The last drawing shows the north of Boston with Noddle Island in the background, and on the left foreground the Mill Pond enclosed by a dyke, and which was later to be filled in with the earth collected from the levelling of Beacon Hill in 1811.

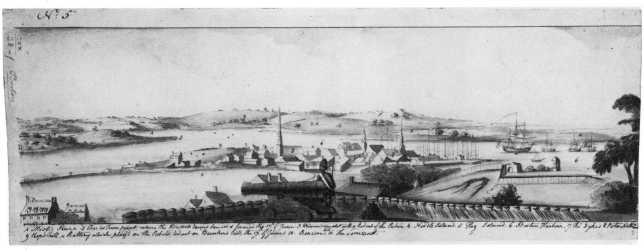

Behold the Yankies in there Ditch's
Whose Conscience gives such griping twitch's
They'r ready to Be S—t their Brech's. Yankie Doodle &c
Next see the Hypocritic parson
Who thay all wish to torn on A—s on
Altho' the Devil keps the farce on. Yankie &c

The
Yankie Doodles
Intrenchments
Near Boston 1776
Publish'd as the Act
Directs

See Putnam that Commands in Chief Sir
Who looks & Labours like a thief sir
To get them daily Bread & Beef sir. Yankie &c
Their Congress now is quite disjoint'd
Since Gibbitsis for them appointed
For fighting gainst y'ʳ Lords Annointed. Yankie doodle

59

## 59 American Defences

The Yankie Doodles Intrenchments near Boston
1776. Published as the Act Directs.

20 × 24cm

*BM Department of Prints and Drawings, Satires* 5329

One of the few satires hostile to the Americans,
this cartoon depicts the militia defending one of
the numerous trenches, fronted by pallisades,
which surrounded Boston. The artist was
apparently unaware that Washington, and not
Putnam, was Commander-in-Chief of the Continental Army.

The hesitant attitude of the American towards
fortifying the country around Boston, which
prevailed prior to the Battle of Bunker Hill, was
soon reversed afterwards when the militia poured
into the American camp. Work began on the
night of the battle to transform gardens and
agricultural land into formidable defences.
Rumours that 'the regulars were coming out'
were to alarm the Americans on several occasions. Intrenchments were thrown up on the
surrounding hills and the British army, pinned
down on Boston, responded by discharging shot
and shells at intervals.

## 60 Yankee Doodle

A Selection of Scotch, English, Irish and Foreign Airs Adapted to the Fife, Violin or German-Flute. Glasgow, Printed and sold by James Aird [1782]. Volume First.

12cm

*BL Music Library a.27*

The words for 'Yankee Doodle' are thought to have originated in 1745, and many variations became well known during the rest of the eighteenth century. There was little printing of secular music in the colonies until the late 1780s, and it is thought that the earliest printing of the music for 'Yankee Doodle' may have been in the first volume of *A Selection of Scotch, English, Irish and Foreign Airs*, first printed in August 1782 by James Aird. The tune without words and under the title 'Yanky Doodle', appears on page 36 of this example of the second issue of Aird's work.

## 61 George Washington (1732–99)

George Washington, Esqr. General and Commander in Chief of the Continental Army in America. Done from an Original, Drawn from the Life by Alexr. Campbell. Published as the Act directs, 9 Septr. 1775 by C. Shepherd.

36 × 26cm

*BM Department of Prints and Drawings, Satires 5290*

Appointed General and Commander-in-Chief of the 'Army of the United Colonies', Washington a wealthy Virginian landowner, received his commission from the second Continental Congress on 17 June 1775, the same day as the Battle of Bunker Hill. This Congress had begun sitting in Philadelphia on 10 May, all thirteen colonies being represented for the first time. Appeals were made by the Massachusetts Bay representatives for Congress to assume the responsibility for directing and maintaining the provincial army surrounding Boston. On 14 June Congress took a decisive step in uniting the actions of the colonies, by voting that six companies of rifle-men be raised in Pennsylvania, and two each in Maryland and Virginia. These were to join the army at Boston. On 15 June it was voted that 'a General be appointed to command all the Continental Forces, raised, or to be raised for the Defence of American Liberty'. Elected by unanimous ballot, Washington was offered five hundred dollars a month for pay and expenses, which he refused saying, 'as no pecuniary Consideration could have tempted me to accept this arduous Employment, at the Expense of my domestic Ease and Happiness, I do not wish to make any Profit from it. I will keep an exact Account of my Expenses. These I doubt not they [Congress] will discharge.' Anxious that his abilities and military experience might not prove equal to the tasks of a Commander-in-Chief he stated to Congress, 'lest some unlucky Event should happen unfavourable to my Reputation, I beg it may be remembered by every Gentleman in the Room, that I this Day declare with the utmost Sincerity, I do not think myself equal to the Command I am honoured with.'

Alexander Campbell, the author of the original painting from which this engraving was taken, was then an unknown artist. Washington wrote on 31 January 1776: 'Mr Campbell, whom I never saw to my knowledge, has made a very formidable figure of the Commander-in-Chief, giving him a sufficient portion of terror in his countenance.' (see p. 101.)

## 62 American Military Instructions, 1775

Military Instructions for officers detached in the field: containing a scheme for forming a Corps of a Partisan. Illustrated with Plans of the Manoeuvres necessary in carrying on the Petite Guerre. By Roger Stevenson. Philadelphia, 1775.

18 × 11cm

*BL Department of Printed Books* 534.c.12

Believed to be the first book dedicated to Washington, it is also one of the earliest American texts on the art of warfare. There was no American Army at the beginning of the War of Independence. Only colonial militia, especially the Massachusetts Army, took the field against Britain's regulars during the early hostilities. George III's professional army, product of the eighteenth-century military system, was confronted by thousands of 'embattled farmers'. Initially lacking in training and discipline, although able to handle firearms, the Americans confined their military manoeuvres to skirmishing in woods or digging in on a strong position. 'We must learn to use other weapons than the pick or spade', said John Adams, 'our armies must be disciplined and learn to fight.'

## 63 Our Cause is Just

A Declaration by the Representatives of the United Colonies of North-America, now met in General Congress at Philadelphia. Seting forth the Causes and Necessity of their taking up Arms. Philadelphia, 1775.

22cm

*BL Department of Printed Books* C.38.f.31.(2)

Having assumed responsibility for directing the course of the revolution, the Second Continental Congress sought a means of inspiring the patriot soldiers at Boston, and others who might join them, with the feeling that they were committed to a cause worthy of their supreme sacrifice. To achieve this aim, and also to persuade the world in general of the justice of resorting to arms, a committee of five, appointed by Congress on 23 June, was assigned the task of drawing up such a declaration. Dissatisfied with the draft produced, Congress appointed to the Committee John Dickinson and Thomas Jefferson, who then wrote the final version. The *Declaration*, approved on 6 July was first printed in Philadelphia on 10 July. A pamphlet edition was published almost immediately by William and Thomas Bradford. Originally intended to have been read publicly by Washington on his arrival at the Boston camp, the *Declaration* was finally communicated to the troops by the president of Harvard. It is notable for the much quoted paragraph, apparently written by Dickinson, which contained a thinly veiled threat to the mother country: 'Our cause is just. Our union is perfect. Our internal resources are great, and if necessary, foreign assistance is undoubtedly available.'

## 64 Great Britain Replies

The Rights of Great Britain Asserted against the Claims of America: being an Answer to the Declaration of the General Congress. The Second Edition. London, Printed for T. Cadell, 1776.

21cm

*BL Department of Printed Books* 8135.cc.9

The *Declaration* provoked several replies in the mother country. The most important response appeared in the pamphlet *The Rights of Great Britain Asserted. against the Claims of America*. Attributed to, among others, James Macpherson, Sir John Dalrymple and Lord George Germain, it appeared anonymously in London in 1776 and went through ten editions. Apparently given every assistance by the Treasury and other government sources, the author, in reply to the assertion that the colonists had established themselves in America 'without any charge to the country from which they removed', produced a table listing a total of £3,835,000 granted to the colonies for the support of civil government and provincial forces in North America. Dismissing the Americans' declaration as having been written, 'with a degree of folly scarce excusable in the most consummate ignorance', the author concluded that, 'Great Britain has obeyed the dictates of humanity beyond the limits prescribed by her reputation. . . . She has long had reason to complain of American ingratitude, and she will not bear longer with American injustice. The dangerous resentment of a great people is ready to burst forth.'

## 65 The Olive Branch Petition

Facsimile of the Olive Branch Petition, 8 July 1775. From the original in HM Public Record Office. London, HMSO, 1934.

23 cm

*BL Official Publications Library B.S.33/9*

Passed in Congress on 8 July, only two days after the approval of the *Causes and Necessity of their taking up Arms,* this petition, written by Dickinson and submitted to the King, was signed by the representatives of all the thirteen colonies. Expressing loyalty to the monarch, its apparent contradiction in terms of the earlier *Declaration* illustrated the deep differences of opinion then held over the fundamental question of separation or reconciliation. The petition described the 'mild and just government' previously prevailing whereby Great Britain and the colonies were 'The wonder and envy of other nations'. All this was endangered by the statutes and regulations imposed on the colonies by his Majesty's ministers. Perceiving 'to their inexpressable astonishment . . . the dangers of a foreign quarrel', the still faithful colonists asked only that the King 'be pleased to direct some mode by which the united applications of your faithful colonists . . . may be improved into a happy and permanent reconciliation'.

Taken from Philadelphia to London by Richard Penn, a copy of the petition was sent to Lord Dartmouth on 21 August. The reply was returned that 'as his Majesty did not receive it on the throne, no answer would be given'. Lord Suffolk commented that: 'The King and his Cabinet are determined to listen to nothing from the illegal congress, to treat with the colonies only one by one, and in no event to recognize them in any form of association.' Released to the press, the petition received enough publicity to ensure its being brought before Parliament when it reconvened on 26 October. The King, in an indirect reply, asserted that the rebels sought, 'only to amuse by vague Expressions of Attachment to the Parent State and the strongest Protestations of Loyalty to Me, whilst they were preparing for a General Revolt'. It was necessary, he said to put, 'a speedy End to these Disorders by the most decisive Exertions'.

## 66 The King's Proclamation of 23 August 1775

By the King, A Proclamation for Suppressing Rebellion and Sedition.

MS

*BL Department of Manuscripts Add.MS 34412. ff. 343–346*

Regarded as officially marking the beginning of the War of Independence, this Proclamation was issued in London on 23 August 1775. Declaring the colonies in North America to be in open rebellion and 'traitorously preparing, ordering and levying War against Us', it obliged all loyal subjects of the King to assist in 'the Supression of such Rebellion, and to disclose and make known all traitorous Conspiracies and attempts against Us, Our Crown and Dignity'. Excluding all hopes of reconciliation, the publication of this Proclamation marked the recognition by the British Ministry that any negotiations would have to be accompanied by the use of force.

This manuscript draft of the Proclamation in its final amended form, is accompanied by a secret letter from North to William Eden, Under-Secretary of State (Northern Department). Describing the difficulty of raising troops, he commented: 'I am, upon the whole, satisfied that their opinion is right who say that if America is ever brought to own the authority of Great Britain, it must be by the Fleet, but I think that a large land force is necessary to render our naval operations effectual.' Concluding his letter, he qualified his remarks saying: 'Upon military matters I speak ignorantly and therefore, without effect. Burn this letter Dear Eden.'

## 67 Boston and Environs

A Plan of Boston in New England with its Environs, Including Milton, Dorchester, Roxbury, Brooklin, Cambridge, Medford, Charlestown, Parts of Maldon and Chelsea. With the Military Works Constructed in those Places in the Years 1775 and 1776. Engrav'd in Agua Tinta by Francis Jukes. London, Published ... June 1st 1777 by Henry Pelham.

1 : 14,100 approx. 2 sh.

122 × 79cm overall

*BL Map Library RUSI A30/26 a and b*

One of the finest maps of Boston of its day, Henry Pelham's plan shows the state of the numerous rebel defence works surrounding the town up to the time of its evacuation in March 1776. Burgoyne, describing the scene to an English friend wrote: 'Look, my Lord, upon the country near Boston – it is all fortification. Driven from one hill you will see the enemy retrenched upon the next and every step we move must be the slow step of a siege.' Pelham, the author of the map, was a Loyalist and was given access to English military maps and sketches. The upper left-hand corner of the map shows Pelham's reproduction of the pass issued to him on 28 August 1775. This gave him authority to visit the front lines to gain information to complete his map. The architecture of war had completely transformed the surrounding countryside. Pelham in a letter of 27 January 1776 to John Singleton Copley, commented: 'An hundred places you might be brought and you not know where you were, I doubt if you would know the town at all. . . . The very hills seem to have altered their form.' This copy of the map, signed by the author, appears to be the earliest engraved state known. The engraved imprint of 1 June 1777 (although

altered in manuscript to 11 June) predates other known copies bearing an imprint of 2 June 1777. The date of the storming of Warren's Redoubt is erroneously given as 17 June 1777 instead of 1775.

## 68 The Occupation of Dorchester Heights

[Map of Boston with six surrounding views.] This Plan and Views of the Capital of New England and Castle of William and Mary in the Harbour of Boston, were taken in the Year 1773, by Lt. Wm. Pierie of the Rl. Regt. of Artillery.

MS 56 × 87cm

*BL Map Library K. Top.CXX.34*

The strategic importance of Dorchester Neck (shown here in the central map), had long been recognized by Washington in formulating his plans for dislodging the British from Boston. He was convinced that by occupying Dorchester Heights and preparing to attack simultaneously from the Cambridge side, he would precipitate a battle. Two thousand men together with 350 carts of tools and prefabricated defences, were therefore marched across the causeway to Dorchester Heights on the night of 4 March 1776. By daylight the following morning, the sixth anniversary of the Boston Massacre, two fortifications had been erected, of which Howe is reported to have said that the provincials had done more work in one night than his whole army would have done in six months. The safety of the troops in Boston, and of the ships in the harbour, was directly threatened. In much the same position as Gage had been in before Bunker Hill, Howe decided to attack Dorchester immediately: 2,400 men under the command of Lord Percy were ordered to Castle William, whence the attack would be launched, but bad weather prevented the British forces from reaching the rendezvous. By the time the storm had cleared the American forces were almost impregnable. Howe's only recourse was to evacuate Boston. For Colour Plate, see p. 19

67

70

**69 Boston Evacuated, 17 March 1776**

Noddle-Island – Or How Are We Deceived.
J.S.sc. London, Pubd. 12 May 1776 by M. Darby.

22 × 16cm

*BM Department of Prints and Drawings, Satires 5335*

Satirizing the evacuation of Boston by Howe on 17 March 1776, this cartoon depicts Americans fighting redcoats, perched on an exaggerated coiffure – a parody of the contemporary hairstyle. The two British flags are decorated with an ass and a fool's cap and bells. On the lower rolls of hair the regulars can be seen rowing towards two ships in full sail. The 'How' in the title is a pun on the Commander-in-Chief's name.

Thomas Newell, a selectman of Boston, wrote of the evacuation: 'Thus was this unhappy distressed town . . . relieved from a set of men whose unparalleled wickedness, profanity, debauchery and cruelty is inexpressible, enduring a siege from 19 April 1775 to the 17 March 1776.'

**70** A copy of a gold medal voted by Congress to General Washington, 25 March 1776, for his 'wise and spirited conduct in the acquisition of Boston'. Engraved by Pierre Simon Duvivier, and struck at the Hôtel des Monnaies, Paris.

*BM Department of Coins and Medals, Betts 542*

# III The Northern Invasions 1775-77

When war broke out in 1775 one major factor in the overall strategic situation was the control of Canada. In British hands Canada was a potential base from which operations could be carried on against the Revolutionaries in New England. Conversely, if the Canadian colonists could be encouraged to join the American side the Revolution would acquire truly continental dimensions.

The part Canada could play in either event was limited: for practical purposes there was a single effective line of communication between Canada and the American colonies. It was possible of course to reach the one from the other by sea, or, as Benedict Arnold did in 1775, through the difficult country along the border to the north of Maine, or along the Mohawk to Lake Ontario; but the economic heart of Canada was the area of Montreal and Quebec. Thus the important route was that from New York to Montreal and Quebec: a ribbon of waterways, it was also the route with the fewest natural obstacles. It passed up the Hudson Valley from New York to Fort Edward. Here there was a choice of a short land crossing to the head of Lake George and thence proceeding by water to Ticonderoga, or of a longer land journey through Skenesborough to Ticonderoga. From Ticonderoga, the route continued by water along Lake Champlain to Fort St John's, and thence either by road to Montreal, or down the River Richelieu to Sorel which lies on the St Lawrence about 100 miles above Quebec. The geographical situation was therefore extremely simple, and events seemed to follow the inevitable course indicated by the lie of the land. In the northern sector of the War the Americans under Montgomery invaded Canada in September 1775. Moving from the base at Ticonderoga, which had been captured from the British the previous May, following Lake Champlain, they captured Fort St John's after a siege of fifty-five days, occupied Montreal and laid siege to Quebec. They retreated along the same line on the arrival of British reinforcements in May 1776.

The British under Burgoyne at once mounted a counter-offensive southwards, of necessity following the same route, with the intention of combining with another British force which, as Burgoyne hoped, was to start from New York and march northwards to execute a pincer movement, crushing the Americans between them. The success of this operation would secure the line of communication between New York and Canada and cut off lateral contact between New England and the other American colonies. It took the British forces marching south two years to penetrate along the line to a point thirty miles north of Albany in the Hudson valley, where they were held up by the Americans, their single line of retreat cut off. Burgoyne was forced to surrender on 17 October 1777.

The reasons for the failure of Burgoyne's expedition have been a source of much speculation. The relationships between the individuals responsible for devising strategy and carrying it out (Germain, Carleton, Howe and Burgoyne) were uneasy, with the result that the force which was sent by Howe from the south to support Burgoyne was too late to prevent defeat. The American approach to tactics was much more flexible than the British in terrain which demanded unconventional methods of warfare. The exact apportionment of responsibility for what happened is still the subject of argument by historians. However, the fundamental cause of failure of both the American invasion northwards and the British invasion southwards must lie in the constricting geographical framework, which channelled all the military operations along a single line.

Finally something must be said of the chief actors in the drama. On each side there was a pair of leaders of contrasting character whose personalities closely influenced the course of events: Carleton and Burgoyne on the British side, Gates and Arnold on the American. Guy Carleton (1724–1808) was Governor of the province of Quebec in 1775 and in the course of the year became commander of the army in Canada. His successes in defending Quebec during the winter of 1775–76 and in organizing the civil government of the province both before and after the War were solid achievements. However, Digby (see no. 76) describes him as 'one of the most distant, reserved men in the world; he has a rigid strictness of manner, very unpleasing and which he observes even to his most particular friends and acquaintance'. John Burgoyne (1722–92) died with no such successes to his credit, but yet, at this time, 'alone engrossed their [the army's] warmest attachment. . . . He possesses a winning manner in his appearance and address, far different from the severity of Carleton, which caused him to be idolized by the army'. Two men of such different temperaments would not have been likely to cooperate in the best of circumstances, but when Burgoyne was given the command of the Canadian army for the campaign of 1777 over Carleton's head, such cooperation became a near impossibility.

Horatio Gates (1728–1806) superseded Schuyler after Burgoyne's capture of Ticonderoga in 1777. He is said to have been indolent and to have attained his success in defeating Burgoyne partly through the strategic advantages of the geographical situation, which have already been discussed, and partly through the vigour of Benedict Arnold (1741–1801), whose character is epitomized by his dramatic march through Maine to Quebec. Here again was an uneasy personal relationship; but the immediate achievements of the partnership were nothing but beneficial for the Americans.

## 71 The Invasion of Canada

An Authentic Journal of Occurrences which happened within the Circle of Major [Return Jonathan] Meigs's Observations, in the Detachment commanded by Col. (now General) Benedictine Arnold. Illustrated with 'A View of the Rivers Kenebec and Chaudiere with Colonel Arnold's Route to Quebec'.

*In*: *London Magazine*, London: R. Baldwin, [1776] Vol xlv.

18 × 11cm

*BL Department of Printed Books PP.* 5437

In September 1775 the Americans launched a two-pronged invasion of Canada, in order to encourage the Canadian population to join the American cause; there was in fact widespread sympathy in Canada for the revolutionaries, particularly among the French-speaking Canadians. The main force under General Richard Montgomery advanced from Ticonderoga northwards along the lakes towards Montreal, while the second force under Benedict Arnold took a route which passed from the headwaters of the Kennebec in Maine across the Boundary Mountains to Lake Mégantic and thence down the Chaudière to emerge at Point Lévis on the St Lawrence opposite Quebec. The country along the march was wild, wet and woody; progress was often as little as three miles a day. In the latter part of the march the force suffered from a serious shortage of provisions and there were some deaths from starvation. Meigs's concise account of the expedition includes an account of the siege of Quebec down to 31 December, when he was taken prisoner. His account of the siege is a useful complement to Danford's (see no. 73) in that the same occurrences are described by both but are seen from opposing points of view. We know from Danford that Meigs acted as an intermediary, after being taken prisoner, so that arrangements could be made with the Americans for the prisoners' baggage to be sent into the city. He was eventually exchanged and, after a varied career, he was appointed by President Jefferson to be US agent amongst the Cherokee Indians in 1801. He held that post until his death in 1823.

## 72 Montreal

A View of the City of Montreal in Canada taken from the top of the Mountain. By James Peachey. Taken 15th Octr. 1784.

Watercolour on paper. 40 × 60cm

*BL Map Library K. Top. CXIX.* 42.*b*

Montreal did not play an important part in the American War of Independence. The Governor of Canada, General Sir Guy Carleton, wisely decided to abandon the city in the face of the American advance under Montgomery, and to concentrate his defence at Quebec. The Americans in their turn abandoned Montreal and retreated to Fort St John's on the Richelieu when Carleton marched out of Quebec in May 1776 with the reinforcements which had newly arrived from England. James Peachey, the artist both of the present view and of the view of Quebec (see no. 75), executed many views of Canada between 1781 and 1793, where he was an officer on the staff of the Director of Surveys for British North America (Samuel Holland) and, later, Deputy Surveyor-General.

## 73 The Siege of Quebec

J. Danford's Book of Memorandums on the Siege and Blockade of Quebec by the Rebels under the Command of Richard Montgomery [and] Benedict Arnold. 1775–76.

MS 17 × 12cm

*BL Department of Manuscripts Add. MS* 46840, *ff.* 34*b*–35

John Danford was a member of the garrison at Quebec, but nothing else is known about him. The diary begins on 10 November 1775: 'Arnold arrived at Point Levy with 500 men which he brought thro' woods from the rebel army at Bouton.' On 14 November they 'crossed the river St Lawrence and showed themselves to the

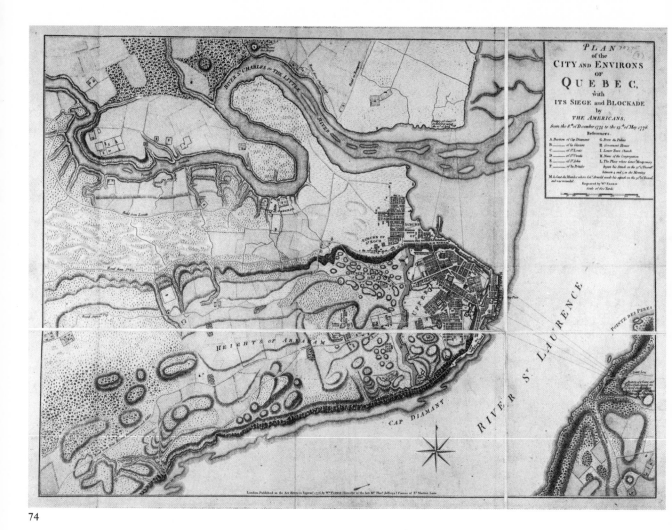

74

garrison. We burnt 3 houses in the Suburbs of Saint Louis Gate.' The diary continues in this laconic style, recording the occurrences of each day. The most important event of the siege, the repulse of the American attack on 31 December, is treated at some length: 'This morning the enemy threw in a great quantity of shells about $\frac{1}{4}$ before 5. An alarm was gave [sic] the enemy having attacked Sault de Matelot with 600 men under the command of Colonel Arnold. . . . An attack was likewise made by 700 men under the command of Genl. Montgomery at Pres de Ville after sending about 200 men to make a feint at Cape Diamond and Saint Johns, but our cannon made them soon retire. He drew up his men on Mr Drummond's wharf and sent an officer to reconnoitre the Barrier who advanced almost to touch it . . . then about 50 of them advanced to a narrow pass facing the Barrier and were within 20 yards of it when they received a general discharge of Cannon and Musquetry which mowed them down like grass . . .' It was at this point that Montgomery was killed.

Another important occurrence took place on 6 May: 'This morning about 6 o'clock the Garrison was alarmed a vessel appearing near the Church of Point Levy. Upon her passing the point she fired 5 Guns and hoisted St George's Ensign which was answered from the Garrison it being the Signal agreed upon that it was a British Vessel. About 7 o'clock she came to an anchor and proved to be the *Surprize* Frigate –

Captn. Lindzay from Plymouth with a company of the 29th Regiment . . .' Thus ended the six months of siege. The Americans retreated in the face of the reinforcements and did not venture into Canada again during the War.

The diary passed through various hands in the nineteenth century and was presented to the British Museum in 1948. Similar accounts of the siege have been published by the Literary and Historical Society of Quebec.

**74** Plan of the City and Environs of Quebec, with its Siege and Blockade by the Americans from the 8th December 1775 to the 13th May 1776.
Engraved by Wm. Faden. London: W^m Faden, 12 Septemb^r, 1776.

1:7,200 45 × 62cm

*BL Map Library* 70775.(3)

John Danford's diary of the siege of Quebec is well illustrated by Faden's map which marks clearly the location of the key events: the place on the opposite bank of the St Lawrence where Arnold made his dramatic appearance on 10 November after his march across the mountains; Près de Ville and Sault de Matelot (letters L and M) where the unsuccessful attacks were launched by the Americans on 31 December.

**75** A View of the City of Quebec the Capital of Canada taken from the Ferry House on the Opposite Side of the River. By James Peachey. Taken Octr. 3d. 1784.

Watercolour on paper. 39 × 60cm

*BL Map Library K. Top. CXIX.39.d*

The view shows the city as seen from near Point Lévis, where Arnold and his detachment appeared on 10 November 1775. On Peachey, see no. 71 above.

**76 William Digby's Account of the British Invasion from the North**

Some Account of the American War between Great-Britain and her Colonies. Wm. Digby, lieut. 53 Regt. 1776–77.

MS 22 × 19cm

*BL Department of Manuscripts Add. MS 32413, ff.90b–91*

William Digby's diary is to some extent complementary to the diary of John Danford: Danford's diary ceases at the relief of Quebec in May 1776; Digby was a member of the relieving forces. Thus the two documents provide between them a continuous eye-witness account of events in the northern sector of operations from the beginning of the siege of Quebec until the capitulation at Saratoga two years later. However unlike Danford's bare record of occurrences, Digby's diary is designed to be read by 'the partial eye of a particular friend'; he sets his intentions out in a brief preface: 'The only merit . . . I can claim is a strict adherence to truth inserted without exagiration [*sic*], and facts set down plainly as they happened . . .' He goes on to say: 'It would exceed the bounds I at first prescribed to enter into the grand causes which actuate a General in the manoeuvres and movements of an army; the impossibility of such an attempt must appear evident to every person. . . . I have confined myself to simple occurrences such as were publicly known to the Army in general.' Thus the journal is for the most part free from the political motivation of many other accounts of Burgoyne's expedition, which sought to incriminate or excuse Burgoyne for his failure.

The diary is exhibited at ff.90b–91, Digby's entry for 17 October 1777, the day of the surrender at Saratoga: 'Thus ended all our hopes of Victory, Honour, Glory, etc. Thus was Burgoyne's unfortunate army sacrificed to the opinions of a blundering Ministerial Power; The stupid inaction of a General who from his lethargic disposition neglected every step he might have taken to assist their operations; or lastly perhaps his own misconduct in penetrating as far as to be unable to return.'

Little is known of Digby: he joined the 53rd Regiment of Foot in 1770 as an ensign and was promoted lieutenant in 1773; after the surrender

76

at Saratoga, he was paroled as a prisoner of war and in 1785 is found in Canada on garrison duty, when he retired on half pay. He retired completely in 1786. The diary was purchased by the British Museum in 1884, and was published with copious annotations by J. P. Baxter in 1887 (*The British Invasion from the North*, Albany, 1887).

### 77 The Campaign of 1776

A Survey of Lake Champlain including Lake George, Crown Point and St. John Surveyed by Order of His Excellency Major-General Sir Jefferey Amherst ... by William Brassier [Brasier], Draughtsman. 1762.

London: Sayer and Bennett, 1776.

1:250,000

65 × 48cm

*BL Map Library* 1. *TAB*. 44. (22)

Brasier's survey covers the key central section of the natural route from the St Lawrence to the Hudson Valley along the lakes, which was the theatre of Carleton and Burgoyne's operations in 1776. St John's, at the top of the map, was retaken on 18 June, after which operations were held up while a fleet was prepared with which to advance south along Lake Champlain. This was ready by the beginning of October, and on 11 October the American fleet was defeated in the strait between Isle de Valcour and the west shore of the lake. The British then quickly advanced to Crown Point, but no further. Because of the approach of winter, the capture of Fort Ticonderoga was left for the following year's campaign.

Brasier's survey was made in connection with the British advance northwards towards the St Lawrence during the Seven Years' War, but this copy was printed when the area again became topical in 1776. Two other maps by Brasier are included in the exhibition: his plans of Crown Point and Fort Ticonderoga (nos. 83, 84). He served as draughtsman and surveyor for the engineering establishment from 1758 to 1774.

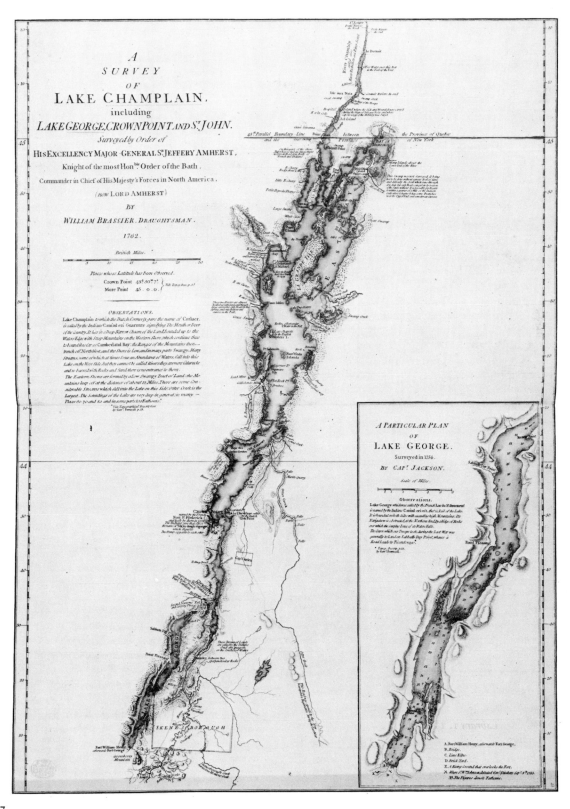

**78 Fort St John's**

Plan of Fort St Iohn on the River Chambly [i.e. Richelieu]. [Signed by] Gother Mann, Quebec 7th May 1791

MS 1:2400

49 × 68cm

*BL Map Library K. Top. CXIX.43.3*

When the American force under Montgomery invaded Canada in September 1775, Fort St John's was the first obstacle in its path. Not until Fort Chambly, the next post to the North, had surrendered was Montgomery able to gain possession of the necessary equipment to force the garrison of St John's to capitulate. Its position on the route from New York along the Hudson Valley to Canada was of the utmost strategic importance, since here the roads diverged to Montreal and Quebec. After the relief of Quebec in May 1776, the Americans retired from Quebec and Montreal to St John's, and from there to Crown Point. The fort was reoccupied by the British under Burgoyne on 18 June, and was used as the base for the preparation of the fleet, without which an advance along the Lakes was impossible.

This plan was drawn at a time when the fort had assumed a new significance as the frontier post on the boundary between Canada and the now independent United States.

**79** A View of St. John's upon the River Sorell [i.e. Richelieu], in Canada, with the Redoubts, Works, &c. taken in the Year 1776, during the late War in America. By Thomas Anburey.

In: T. Anburey, *Travels through the Interior Parts of America*, London, 1789.

25 × 41cm

*BL Department of Printed Books* 1052.e.13

Thomas Anburey served as a volunteer in the 29th Foot in Burgoyne's army, and during his service wrote the successful *Travels through the Interior Parts of America* in the form of a series of letters to a friend, with illustrations. He writes of his plan of Fort St John's: 'I have enclosed you a drawing of it representing the two redoubts, with the rope-walk, the ship [the *Inflexible*, which was knocked down to pieces at Montreal and re-assembled by sixteen shipwrights at St John's in twenty-eight days; see no. 80] on the stocks and the other vessels at anchor near the fort and which I have taken from the block-house erected on the opposite side of the river Sorell.' The block-house is marked on the plan of the fort, no. 78. Conventional stylized groups of Indians are placed in the foreground.

**80 Naval Operations on Lake Champlain**

The Attack and Defeat of the American Fleet under Benedict Arnold, by the Kings Fleet Commanded by Captn. Thos. Pringle upon Lake Champlain, the 11th October 1776. Engraved by Wm. Faden from a Sketch taken by an Officer on the Spot.

London: Wm. Faden, 1776.

1:80,000

48 × 46cm

*BL Map Library* 70220.(2)

One of the great problems facing Carleton in his advance south after the retreating Americans was the need for vessels with which to transport his army along Lake Champlain and to attack the fleet which the Americans had mustered on the lake. Prefabricated boats were built, carried along the Richelieu past the rapids and reassembled at St John's (see nos. 78 and 79). The delay caused by this operation was seen later as a contributory factor to the disaster of Saratoga; yet without the boats, the advance could not have taken place. The fleet eventually comprised twenty gun-boats, 680 flat-bottomed boats, two schooners (the *Carleton* and *Maria*), a 'radeau' with sixteen guns (the *Thunderer*), a 'gondola' (the *Royal Convert*) which had been captured from the Americans, and the *Inflexible*, a square-rigged three-master with eighteen guns. The fleet met the Americans at a point about forty-eight miles north of Crown Point on 11 October 1776. The

American fleet had taken up a position in the narrow strait between the Isle de Valcour and the west shore of the lake, but it was quickly defeated by the superior gun power of the British squadron. However, during the night, the Americans effected an escape through the British line and retired to Ticonderoga (abandoning Crown Point), where they remained until July the following year.

**81** Naval Engagement on Lake Champlain 11 Oct. 1776. By Henry Gilder.

Watercolour on paper. 25 × 36cm

*Lent by Her Majesty the Queen, by whose gracious permission it is reproduced.*

*Windsor Castle Inventory of Drawings no.* 17849.

Gilder's drawing of the Naval Squadron on Lake Champlain apparently represents the same stage in the engagement as Faden's plan (no. 80). The key to the explanatory letters on the drawing has been revealed recently during remounting and is as follows:

a  Cumberland Head
b  Cumb.ᵈ Bay
c  I. de Valcour
d  Petite Isle
e  Grande Isle
f  Rebel Fleet
g  Carleton Schooner
h  Royal Savage aground
i  Line of Gun Boats
k  Inflexible
l  Maria
m  Royal Convert
n  Thunderer Radeau

The situation of the American fleet shows that it had little chance against the British attack.

Henry Gilder was a pupil of Thomas Sandby and exhibited at the Royal Academy in 1773, 1774, 1776, 1778. This makes it unlikely that the present drawing was taken on the spot; it may well have been worked up from the sketch on which Faden's plan is based.

For Colour Plate, see p. 20

**82 The Campaign of 1777**

A Topographical Map of Hudson's River . . . and the Country adjacent, from Sandy-Hook, New York and Bay to Fort Edward, also the Communication with Canada by Lake George and Lake Champlain, as high as Fort Chambly on Sorel River. By Claude Joseph Sauthier, on the Original Scale of Four Miles to One Inch. Engraved by William Faden.
London: Wm. Faden, Octʳ. 1st 1776.

1:250,000. 79 × 52cm

*BL Map Library* 73956.(2)

Sauthier's map illustrates the ground covered by Burgoyne in 1777. Towards the end of June the army reached Crown Point where Carleton had turned back the previous year. Fort Ticonderoga was taken on 6 July, when the Americans abandoned it and retired along the road to Skenesborough, obstructing the way with felled trees as they went. At this point Burgoyne began to lose his advantage. The slow progress of the army in the face of the obstructions, the subsequent defeat of an expedition sent to capture American supplies at Bennington (not shown on the map), the failure of Howe to mount an adequate supporting operation from the south, and the discovery that the local population were not Loyalists to the extent that had been supposed, were among the factors which combined to convert Burgoyne's offensive momentum to a defensive standstill which culminated in the capitulation at Saratoga on 17 October.

**83 Crown Point**

Plan of the Fortress and dependant Forts at Crown Point with their Environs and part of Lake Champlain. Survey'd & drawn by Wm Brasier. 1759.

MS 1:7200 approx. 79 × 107cm

*BL Department of Manuscripts Add. MS* 57713.4

Crown Point lies on the western shore of Lake Champlain about fifteen miles north of Ticonderoga. On this site in 1731 the French had built

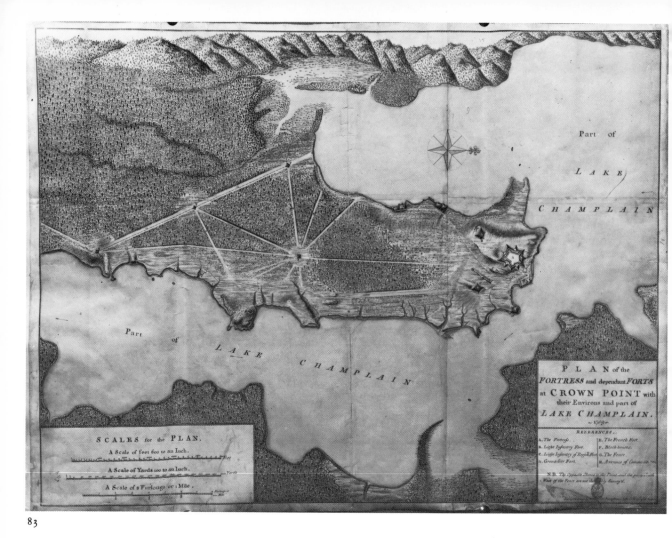

Fort St Fréderic, which was captured in 1759 by Amherst, British Commander-in-Chief, during the Seven Years' War. Strategically the fort was treated as an outpost of Fort Ticonderoga, and following the American capture of Ticonderoga in May 1775 it was quickly taken in its turn, having a garrison of just twelve men. Crown Point was abandoned by the Americans in the following year, after their defeat at the hands of the British squadron on 11 October. Carleton did not put a British garrison into the fort but retired to winter quarters on the St Lawrence. In 1777 Burgoyne launched his attack on Ticonderoga from Crown Point.

The plan gives a graphic impression of the thickly wooded terrain of the area, which greatly impeded movement by land. An archaic feature of the plan is the depiction of the horizon in pro-

file. The plan belonged to Amherst, and passed with his map collection to the Royal United Service Institution, and thence, in 1968, to the British Museum.

## 84 Fort Ticonderoga

A Survey of the Fort at Tienderoga and its Environs, with the French Lines and part of Lake Champlain. 1759. The Fort and lines by Lieut. Brheam, Asst. Enginr:, the Ground Survey'd November 1759 by W: Brasier, Draughtsman to the Ch: Engineer. W. Brasier fecit.

MS 1:4800 approx. 65 × 70cm

*BL Department of Manuscripts Add. MS 57712.10*

Fort Ticonderoga, situated at the point where the waters from Lake George passed into Lake

*A View of TICONDEROGA from a Point on the North Shore of Lake Champlain.*

85

Champlain, had been built by Montcalm in 1756, but was captured by Amherst in 1759 on his advance from the south to the St Lawrence. Captured by the Americans in May 1775, in order to gain possession of equipment and guns to press the siege of Boston, the fort was the base from which Montgomery's invasion of Canada was launched in September of the same year. Its recapture by Burgoyne in July 1777 provided a great boost to British morale. The success of the operation opened the passage to Fort Edward in the Hudson Valley, and so on to Albany, where it was intended to join troops advancing from New York.

The plan is a companion piece to the plan of Crown Point (no. 83) and exhibits many of the same cartographic characteristics. Sugar Hill, the possession of which was the key factor in the success of Burgoyne's attack on the fort (see no. 86), lies to the bottom left of the plan. (From the RUSI collection.)

**85** A View of Ticonderoga from a Point on the North Shore of Lake Champlain. By James Hunter. 1777.
Watercolour on paper. 34 × 42cm
*BL Map Library K. Top. CXXI. 107.b*

The view apparently shows the situation prior to the attack on Fort Ticonderoga on 6 July

1777. The fort lies in the middle distance at the centre of the drawing, which shows some of the works marked on Brasier's plan (no. 84). The boom seen lying across the water protected the American fleet and is described by Digby: 'The enemy, with their usual industry, had joined those two posts [the fort and Mount Independence] by a bridge of communication thrown over the inlet . . . a great and laborious work . . . It was defended by a boom composed of very large pieces of timber fastened together by riveted bolts, and double chains made of iron an inch and a half square. Thus . . . all access by water from the Northern side was totally cut off.' In accordance with artistic conventions of the time a pair of Indians has been included in the foreground, as in Anburey's view of St John's (see no. 79).

**86** *London Gazette*, special edition, 25 August 1777.

32 × 20cm

*BL Department of Manuscripts Add. MS* 39190, *ff.*233–234.

The issue comprises a despatch from Burgoyne to Lord George Germain giving an account of the capture of Fort Ticonderoga on 6 July. The attack had been launched from Crown Point (see no. 83) and was immediately successful, largely because the Americans had decided to leave Sugar Hill unfortified, and this commanded the fort from the south-west. They had not anticipated that the British would be able to establish a post on the summit because of the steep slopes of the hill. On 5 July the British confounded the Americans by moving up their artillery to the summit. Fort Ticonderoga was so vulnerable from this quarter that the Americans abandoned it by night at once, with the British in pursuit. Digby writes: 'We continued the pursuit the whole day without any sort of provisions (and indeed I may say we had very little or none excepting one cow we happened to kill in the woods which without bread was next to nothing among so many).' With this operation the suc-

cessful phase of Burgoyne's invasion came to an end.

**87 Stillwater**

Plan of the Position of the Army under the command of Lieut. Genl. Burgoyne near Still Water, in which it encamped on ye. 20th. Septr. 1777.

MS 1:7200 approx. 53 × 71cm

*BL Department of Manuscripts Add. MS* 57715.5

The period between the capture of Fort Ticonderoga and the encampment of Burgoyne's army at Stillwater witnessed a radical change in Burgoyne's situation. He had taken until the end of July to reach the Hudson at Fort Edward, because of the obstructions caused by the Americans along the road through Skenesborough, and, having reached it, he delayed until he had collected sufficient supplies to proceed down the Hudson. The defeat at Bennington brought the first actual reverse in the two years' campaigns since the relief of Quebec. A second British setback was the successful stand of the Americans at Fort Stanwix along the Mohawk River against the advance of a British detachment under Col. Barry St Leger from Lake Ontario towards the Hudson. Burgoyne's army found itself confined in the Hudson Valley with overstretched lines of communication back to Canada and with the country on either side of the valley under the control of the American militia. On 13 September Burgoyne advanced from Fort Edward across the Hudson and on 19 September attacked the main American force (which had been encamped at Stillwater) at Bemis Heights. The result was indecisive, although the British claimed a victory. Digby describes the engagement: 'The crash of cannon and musketry never ceased until darkness parted us, when they retired to their camp, leaving us masters of the field; but it was a dear bought victory if I can give it that name, as we lost many brave men.' Anburey echoes Digby: 'Notwithstanding the glory of the day remains on our side, I am fearful the real advantages re-

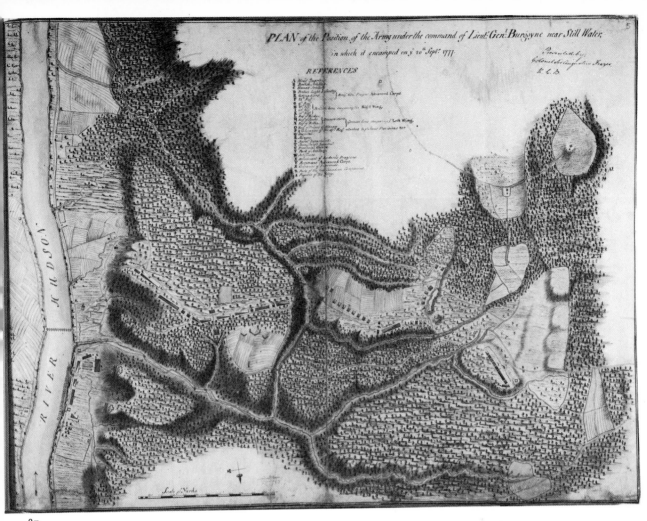

PLAN of the Position of the Army under the command of Lieut. Genl. Burgoyne near Still Water,
in which it encamped on yr 20th Septr. 1777

REFERENCES

sulting from this hard-fought battle, will rest on that of the Americans.' The British army remained at Stillwater until 7 October.

The author of the map is not known. Wilkinson's map of the camp, engraved and published by Faden in 1780, and included in Burgoyne's *Expedition from Canada* (no. 91) includes the American camp to the south and shows rather less ground to the north. (From the RUSI collection.)

**88** The burial of Brig.-Gen. Simon Fraser, 8th Oct. 1777. By John Graham (1754–1817), Scottish school.

Oil on canvas laid on a wood panel. 70 × 92cm

*Lent by the National Army Museum*

On 7 October Burgoyne, who had been encamped at Stillwater since 20 September, attempted a final thrust against the Americans. The fighting was fierce and prolonged, but the outcome was conclusive: Burgoyne lost 600 men and ten guns. Much of the credit for the American success was due to the vigour of Benedict Arnold. One of the three members of Burgoyne's general staff, Simon Fraser, was mortally wounded by a shot in the intestines and died the following morning. Digby describes the funeral: 'At sunset Gen. Frazier was buried, according to his desire, & General Burgoyne attended the service, which was performed I think in the most solemn manner I ever before saw; perhaps the scene around, big with the fate of many, caused it to appear more so . . .' This defeat sealed the fate of Burgoyne's army. It began its retreat at 11 pm that evening.

### 89 Surrender at Saratoga

Fresh Important Intelligence Received this Morning, Baltimore, 2 November 1777. Printed by John Dunlap.

40 × 7cm

*BL Department of Manuscripts Add. MS* 34414, *f.* 389

After the failure of Burgoyne's final attempt to advance from Stillwater on 7 October, there was no alternative to a retreat. Burgoyne fell back to Saratoga on the 8th, with the intention of retiring to Fort Edward. Delaying his departure from Saratoga until 12 October, he found his army completely surrounded by the Americans under Gates and had no choice but to surrender. Following a series of negotiations, a convention was signed on 17 October, under which the British troops were granted the honours of war. It was intended that the troops should be transported back to England, on condition that none of them should serve again in America; in the event they remained in America as prisoners of war until the end of hostilities.

The news of Saratoga reached Baltimore some two weeks afterwards, as is evident from this news-sheet; it reached London via Canada on 2 December and Paris shortly afterwards. This news encouraged the French, and later the Spaniards and the Dutch, to enter the War on the American side.

90 Letter of Lord George Germain to William Eden, Under-Secretary of State (Northern Department), 3 December 1777.

MS Autograph. 24 × 18cm

*BL Department of Manuscripts Add. MS* 34414, *f.*394

When the news of Saratoga reached London late on 2 December, consternation spread through the Government. Eden's superior, Lord Suffolk, sent him the following terse note: 'Your good reports have been sadly verified! Burgoyne has been forced to capitulate on condition of being embarked with the Remains of his army at Boston for Britain! This news won't help to digest your supper – therefore I hope this is not the first Tidings you have had of it.' The next morning Germain writes to Eden: 'I feel so anxious that some measures should be agreed upon in the present unfortunate situation that I cannot help asking you whether you know anything of Lord North this morning, and whether in the night he has slept, or instead of it, has thought of any Expedient for Extricating this Country out of its distress. I can think and speak of nothing but America, we must have recourse in my poor opinion to a sea war taking proper posts, and carrying attacks along the Coasts of the Rebels with three or four thousand troops to land occasionally in assistance of the Naval operations. Whoever commands must have full power to treat, and Parliament must give its sanction to Ministry for that purpose.'

91 A state of the Expedition from Canada as laid before the House of Commons by Lieutenant-General Burgoyne and verified by evidence; with a collection of authentic documents and an addition of many circumstances which were prevented from appearing before the House by the pro-rogation of Parliament. London: J. Almon, 1780.

27cm

*BL Department of Printed Books* 194.*a*.19

Saratoga marked the turning of the War in the Americans' favour. In England there was naturally much agitation, with the conduct of the War in general, and of Burgoyne's expedition in particular, called into question. Burgoyne was permitted by the Americans to return to England on parole in May 1778, and in 1779 a parliamentary select committee was set up to examine the state of the army which had surrendered. Burgoyne felt that he was unfairly treated by this committee and wrote *A State of the Expedition from Canada* as a *pièce justificative*. In it he provides a narrative of events, publishes the proceedings of the committee, discusses them, and, in a 'Conclusion', blames his defeat on mismanagement by Lord George Germain, in that Germain failed to ensure that Howe in the south and Carleton in the north provided the necessary cooperation and support, and that he did not allow Burgoyne any latitude to vary the plan of campaign which had been laid down from London. It is true that if Howe had played his part in executing the planned pincer movement, the outcome of the campaign, and indeed of the whole War, might have been different; and that if Burgoyne, when he was faced with such uncertain odds at Fort Edward, had felt able to disobey his instructions to advance to Albany and had instead sensibly retreated to Ticonderoga, the worst of the ensuing misfortunes might have been avoided. Nevertheless, Burgoyne was guilty of some serious miscalculations after the capture of Ticonderoga, which place a good measure of the blame for the outcome on his shoulders.

92

**92 American powder horn c.1770**

Made of cow horn and engraved with a map of the Mohawk and Hudson rivers, the royal arms and a view of New York.

*Lent by HM Tower of London. Armouries Inventory Number XIII 126*

# IV *The War in the Middle Colonies* 1775-78

The Patriot cause made less headway at first in the middle and southern colonies than in New England, partly because the former possessed a greater number of loyalists and partly because there were no extensive early clashes with British troops in those areas, apart from in New York. The British had concentrated their coercive measures largely in Boston and New England and the Loyalists elsewhere remained an influential body for much of the War. Few people wanted complete independence from Britain in 1775; a writer in the *New Hampshire Gazette* in August believed '*scarcely ten Men in America*' wanted this. At the same time, however, colonial assemblies were gradually assuming the functions of the Governor and his council, while Britain was showing no signs of changing her intransigent attitude towards the thirteen colonies. With the calling-out of the militia and the invasion of Canada, when Americans were fighting British troops, loyalty to the Crown became increasingly anachronistic. Such events, together with the writings of patriot pamphleteers such as Tom Paine, Samuel Adams and Charles Lee, made the cause of Independence more popular with the public; Paine's *Common Sense* (1776) was of major importance in promoting the patriot cause. John Adams in April 1776 saw Independence to be approaching: 'The Colonies are all at this moment turning their eyes that way. Vast majorities in all the colonies now see the propriety and necessity of taking the decisive steps, and those who are averse to it are afraid to say much against it . . .'. The supporters of Independence were greatly heartened by the failure of a British expeditionary force at Fort Sullivan, off Charlestown. Individual colonies proclaimed their independence and, after long debates, the Declaration of Independence was approved in July 1776. This led on to the War which many, including George III, had long seen as inevitable.

Britain in the meantime had failed to intervene effectively in America. The drift to war might have been averted had troops been speedily dispatched to America and had the Government acted in a firm but conciliatory spirit. Instead, Lord North's ministry was reluctant to ask Parliament for the necessary money in the face of radical opposition and public apathy. The public did not rise to the support of the Crown. North found in November 1775 that: 'The ardor of the nation in this cause has not hitherto arisen to the pitch one could wish . . .'. The strenuous efforts of Lord George Germain to send men, provisions, and equipment to America were hampered by administrative and transport difficulties. The Government, moreover, remained uncertain whether to conciliate or conquer the colonists, and in the end attempted both; the Howe brothers were sent both as commanders-in-chief and as peace commissioners. To some extent their desire as peace commissioners to win over the Americans prevented them from acting with sufficient vigour as military leaders. Their attempts to negotiate proved abortive; they arrived in America too late, just as the Declaration of Independence was approved. The British invasion of the middle colonies duly began. The Howes confidently proceeded to carry out their part in the long-considered, attractive but unsound plan to isolate and blockade

New England, the heartland of the rebellion. While the New England ports were to be blockaded, the Howes were to take New York and Rhode Island and link up with a force marching south from Canada, so cutting off New England from the rest of the colonies. For this to succeed in forcing the colonists to come to terms a quick decisive victory was essential over the Continental Army commanded by General Washington. Victory seemed certain as the Americans were considered to be poor soldiers. The 'native American' was called 'an effeminate Thing, very unfit for & very impatient of War'. The colonists were indeed inexperienced in warfare, but they possessed in Washington a leader of no ordinary ability. The Howes defeated him several times but failed to trap him in the open, and to inflict a decisive defeat on the Continental Army. Washington survived the disasters of the 1776 campaign and the rigours of the winter of 1777–78 in his winter quarters at Valley Forge, and successfully countered the slow conventional tactics of General Howe. On occasions too, as at Trenton and Germantown, the hunted struck back effectively at the hunters. American morale rose and the American soldier and militiamen gained in confidence and experience.

The colonists were further helped by a grave tactical error made by General Howe. Howe's responsibility for the disaster at Saratoga is still the subject of debate; it now appears that he did not expect to have to give Burgoyne any assistance from the south on his march from Canada. Howe was nevertheless taking a serious risk in departing for Philadelphia late in the campaign season, thus making it most unlikely that he could return to New York before the season's end, and in leaving Clinton with insufficient troops to render Burgoyne any effective help. The Philadelphia campaign was in any case misguided; the Americans had no established 'capital' and the fall of the seat of Congress could have had no decisive effect on the War, as the British hoped. The plan to encircle New England consequently ended in the disaster at Saratoga. After Saratoga and the near-defeat at Germantown, Howe was driven to resign, aware that two costly campaigns had ended in stalemate. The British army had failed to obtain the expected decisive victory, and it now seemed likely that France would intervene on the side of the Americans, to obtain revenge for her defeat in the Seven Years' War. Lord Shelburne had earlier forecast: 'It is too much to expect that Europe will remain quiet as it does, and the first Spark which either Plan or Accident gives birth to will expose our Weakness, when our Case is desperate.'

## 93 The Theatre of Operations

The Provinces of New York and New Jersey; with part of Pensilvania and the Province of Quebec. Drawn by Cap.$^t$ Holland. Engraved by Thomas Jefferys . . . and Improved by Govern.$^r$ Pownall, . . . 1776. London: Sayer and Bennett, 17th Aug.$^t$ 1776.

1:650,000. 134 × 52cm

*BL Map Library K. Top. CXXI.5*

Inset maps of New York and Amboy, and a chart of the mouth of the Hudson are also shown. The map covers much of the area affected by the campaigns of 1776 and 1777, and illustrates the strategic importance of the area. The British army and navy could co-operate in occupying much of the area. Shelter of a kind, though not as satisfactory as the shelter available at Rhode Island, could be obtained for the fleet, and the army could link up with a force coming from Canada to isolate New England, while the fleet blockaded the American coast. The colonists realized the importance of the Hudson Valley, and Washington guarded the upper Hudson Valley and the Highlands with forts and gun batteries, moving his supply depots behind them; he believed 'the importance of those posts demands the utmost attention, and every intention to maintain them'. The map indicates how Britain could have been tempted to try to isolate New England, and how disaster was always the probable outcome; the British lines would always have been open to attacks from the neighbouring highlands.

## 94 Calling Out the Militia

Appointment, by the Provincial Congress of New York, of Jeremiah Snyder to the rank of First Lieutenant in a militia regiment in Ulster County, N.Y., 2 November 1775.

20 × 30cm

*BL Department of Manuscripts Add. MS 21842, f.292*

The colonial legislatures in 1775 proceeded to call out their militias, the traditional local defence forces both in America and in Britain. These local troops formed an important part of Congress's national defence plans, being sent for short periods to swell the numbers of Washington's army. They frequently proved inexperienced and unreliable; colonies were sometimes reluctant to send them beyond their own borders, and Washington was sometimes hampered late in the campaign season by their returning to their homes. There were other times when they served him well, coming to his aid when his Continental Army was hard-pressed. They were a match for the British troops in mountainous or wooded terrain, proving adept at ambushing, sniping and general harassment of the enemy.

The Provincial Congress of New York first met in May 1775. British troops were withdrawn in June and in October Governor Tryon was forced to take refuge on board the sloop *Halifax*. He remained off New York, a helpless spectator of events, until restored as Governor when the British occupied New York in September 1776.

## 95 'Common Sense'

Common Sense; Addressed to the Inhabitants of America. Philadelphia: Printed and sold by W. and T. Bradford, 1776. 2nd edition.

26cm

*BL Department of Printed Books 8176. bbb.5*

*Common Sense* was first published in Philadelphia in January 1776. A British immigrant, Paine sought to further the cause of independence in America which was still a matter of some dispute. He advocated a confederation of American colonies, for the mutual development of their resources, independent of a Britain incapable of protecting them, which had exploited them for its own economic interests; reconciliation was now impossible.

'Our prayers have been rejected with disdain. . . . No man was a warmer wisher for reconciliation than myself, before the fatal nineteenth of April 1775, but the moment the event of that day was made known, I rejected the hardened, sullen-tempered Pharaoh of [England]

COMMON SENSE;

ADDRESSED TO THE

INHABITANTS

OF

AMERICA,

On the following interesting

SUBJECTS:

I. Of the Origin and Design of Government in general, with concise Remarks on the English Constitution.

II. Of Monarchy and Hereditary Succession.

III. Thoughts on the present State of American Affairs.

IV. Of the present ability of America, with some miscellaneous Reflections.

A NEW EDITION, with several Additions in the Body of the Work. To which is Added an APPENDIX; together with an Address to the People called QUAKERS.

*Man knows no Master save creating* HEAVEN,
*Or those whom choice and common Good ordain.*
THOMSON.

PHILADELPHIA:

PRINTED and SOLD by W. and T. BRADFORD.

M,DCC,LXXVI.

[PRICE ONE BRITISH SHILLING.]

95

for ever, and disdain the wretch, that with the pretended title of FATHER OF HIS PEOPLE can unfeelingly hear of their slaughter, and composedly sleep with their blood upon his soul.'

Paine called for a continental conference to frame a constitutional charter to secure freedom, property, and freedom of worship for all men, anticipating the events of six months later. Some of his arguments were not new; many were repelled by his language; but he expressed succinctly in a popular form the patriots' case for independence, and won wide support. Nicholas Cresswell, a British observer caught in rebel territory, commented on 26 January: 'Nothing but Independence will go down. The Devil is in the people.'

## 96 The Declaration of Independence, 4 July 1776

[Begin:] In Congress, July 4, 1776. The unanimous Declaration of the thirteen united States of America...

Facsimile. 86 × 72cm

*BL Department of Printed Books A.S.288/21*

'We hold these truths to be self-evident, that all men are created equal, that they are endowed by their Creator with certain unalienable Rights, that among these are Life, Liberty and the pursuit of Happiness. That to secure these rights, Governments are instituted among men, deriving their just powers from the consent of the governed.'

Drafted by Thomas Jefferson with the assistance of John Adams and Benjamin Franklin, the *Declaration* was an assertion not only of the ancient claim of those governed, to consent to, or dissent from, the acts of their government, and of the natural rights of man, but also a revolutionary casting aside of a traditional sacred allegiance. The rights of man now included the right to dissolve 'any Form of Government ... destructive of the above rights ... and to institute new Government'. Many were repelled by these claims; others wanted no such manifesto until the war had been won, and state authorities firmly established; but without it no foreign aid was likely. The *Declaration* was, in A. M. Schlesinger's words, 'the ablest piece of propaganda' of the independence controversy, the fruit of the work of Paine, Adams, and the Patriot journalists and pamphleteers. Patriots were spurred on to remove all vestiges of British rule, and to cow loyalists into submission. For the British the *Declaration* dashed all hopes of a peace based on the colonies' submission, the only acceptable condition for a settlement.

DECLARATION OF INDEPENDENCE

96

LA DESTRUCTION DE LA STATUE ROYALE A NOUVELLE YORCK.

*Die Zerstörung der Königlichen Bild Säule zu Neu Yorck.* | *La Destruction de la Statuë royale a Nouvelle Yorck.*

97

### 97 Destruction of the Royal Statue at New York

La Destruction de la Statuë royale a Nouvelle Yorck. Gravé par François Xav. Habermann. Augsbourg [*c*.1776].

28 × 40cm

*BM Department of Prints and Drawings* 1898-7-25-8

A statue of the King had been erected on the Bowling Green after the repeal of the Stamp Act, 1766. Attacks on persons, property and institutions had been perpetrated since the late 1760s, both by the New York Sons of Liberty, and by British soldiers, who in January 1770 had destroyed the New York Liberty Pole. Now in the excitement engendered by the Declaration of Independence and its adoption by the Provincial Congress of New York on 9 July 1776 the royal statue was pulled down. The statue of the Earl of Chatham, a strong advocate of reconciliation, was not touched. This destruction was both a gesture of patriotic triumph and one of defiance, in a city politically divided and threatened with occupation.

## 98 A Call to Arms

An Oration delivered at the State-House in Philadelphia ... The 1st of August 1776. By Samuel Adams. London: re-printed for J. Johnson, 1776.

28cm

*BL Department of Printed Books 103.c.22*

Adams here calls upon all Americans, to reject monarchical power – 'political popery' – and support their constitution and legislature. The alternatives were 'Independence or the most ignominous and galling servitude. The Legions of our Enemies thicken on our plains', Adams wrote, 'whilst the mangled corses of our Countrymen seem to cry out to us as a voice from Heaven ...' With Howe's army poised to attack New York, Adams attacked the still influential loyalists: 'Their number is but few and daily decreases', and extolled, 'the blessings which Providence holds out to us, the *happiness,* the *dignity* of uncontrouled *freedom and Independence*'.

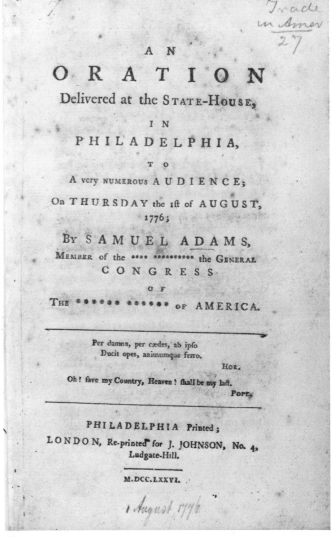

98

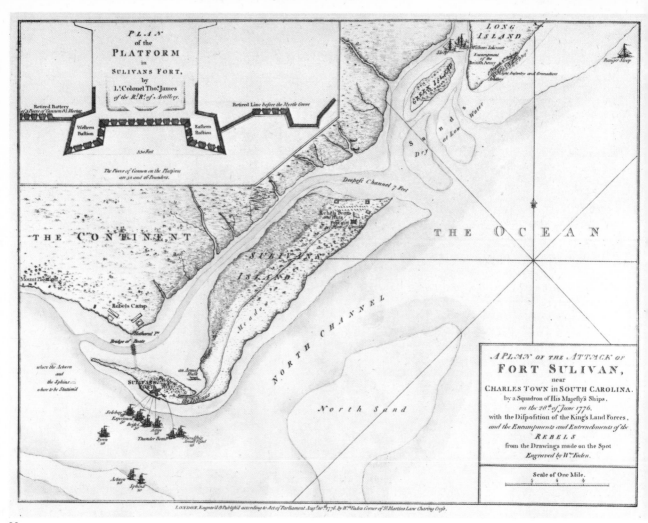

## 99 The First Southern Campaign – Sullivan's Island

A Plan of the Attack of Fort Sulivan, near Charles Town in South Carolina . . . on the 28th of June 1776 . . . Engraved by W<sup>m</sup>. Faden. London: W<sup>m</sup>. Faden, Aug<sup>t</sup> 10th 1776.

1:25,000. 40 × 51cm

*BL Map Library* 1.*TAB*.44.(42)

The American drift towards independence was not checked by an unsuccessful British attack on Fort Sullivan in 1776, undertaken in the mistaken belief, fostered by the former governors of the Southern States, that a British presence would bring about a loyalist counter-revolution. Prompt action in 1775 might have proved more successful, but delayed preparations and con-

trary winds meant that it was May 1776 before the force under Commodore Sir Peter Parker joined General Clinton off Cape Fear, months after the southern Loyalists had been crushed. A large-scale mainland offensive was now impossible, and the Sullivan's Island venture was adopted instead.

This plan was misconceived, for the Charleston area was Patriot country, and well prepared against attack. Even if successful, the venture could not have helped the Loyalists inland. Nevertheless the troops were disembarked on Long Island, whence they were to ford the shallow water between Long and Sullivan's Islands, and join in a sea and land assault on the fort. The plan gives the positions of the opposing forces and also indicates that, as the British

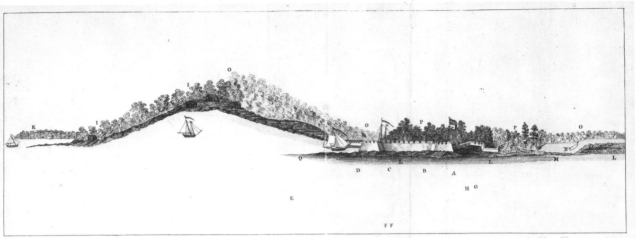

A N.b.E. View of the Fort on the Western end of Sulivans Island with the Disposition of His Majesty's Fleet Commanded by Commodore Sir Peter Parker Knt. &c &c &c. during the Attack on the 28th of June 1776. which lasted 9 hours and 40 minutes.

A. The Active 28 Guns Capt. Williams. B. Briftol Commodore Sir Peter Parker Knt. &c. &c. &c. of 50 Guns, Capt. Morris. C. Experiment 50 Guns Capt. Scot. D. Solebay 28 Guns Capt. Simons. E. Syren 28 Guns Capt. Fourneau. F F. The Acteon of 28 Guns Capt. Atkins and Sphynx of 20 Guns Capt. Hunt on a Shoal the latter got off but the Acteon was burnt by our felves the next Morning as it was impoffible to get her off. G H. The Thunder Bomb Capt. Reed with the Friendfhip Armed Veffel of 28 Guns Capt. Hope. I I Mount Pleafant. K Hog-Ifland. L Sulivans Ifland and Fort. M A Narrow Ifthmus. N. An Armed Hulk to defend the Ifthmus. O The Continent. P. The Myrtle Grove. Q. The Weftern end of Sulivans Ifland & Fort Erected upon a Peninfula.

LONDON. Engrav'd & Publifh'd according to Act of Parliament Aug. 10th 1776. by W. Faden Corner of St Martins Lane Charing Crofs.

100

discovered, the water was too deep to be forded. Furthermore, the crossing was controlled by 800 American troops, and the army was therefore unable to reach the navy stationed off the fort at the southern end of the island.

100 A N. b. E. View of the Fort on the Western end of Sulivan's Island, with the Disposition of his Majesty's Fleet, Commanded by Commodore Sir Peter Parker Knt. . . . during the Attack on the 28th of June 1776 . . . London, W. Faden, Augt. 10th, 1776.

28 × 42cm

*BL Map Library* 72135. (2)

Without any military support, Parker rashly proceeded with his naval attack without consulting Clinton; they had earlier disagreed over tactics. Disaster followed; two vessels sent to attack the fort's unfinished west side ran aground on a shoal; one later had to be destroy-

ed. Two vessels fouled each other, another had to withdraw, and the *Bristol* and *Experiment* were severely damaged, with considerable losses, by accurate enemy fire. British losses were four times the American losses, because the British fire was simply absorbed by the fort's walls of spongy palmetto wood. The attack was abandoned at nightfall, and after days of inactivity the British sailed to join the Howes off New York.

General Lee had nearly abandoned the fort but had been persuaded to defend it. His subsequent vigour gave the Americans heart; his coming was said to be 'equal to a reinforcement of 1,000 men . . . he taught us to think lightly of the enemy and gave a spur to all our actions'.

The south was henceforth left alone for four years. The myth of widespread Loyalist support in the south died hard; this and the earlier Loyalist defeats were simply attributed to the absence of any British troops.

CHARLES LEE, Esqr.

*MAJOR GENERAL of the* CONTINENTAL-ARMY *in* AMERICA.

*Publish'd as the Act directs, 31.Octr. 1775. by C. Shepherd, London.*

101

**101 The Defender of Sullivan's Island**

Charles Lee Esqr. Major General of the Continental Army in America.
Thomlinson pinx. London: C. Shepherd, 1775.

38 × 25cm

*BM Department of Prints and Drawings*
1856-7-12-258

Charles Lee (1731–82) was born in England and saw service in America as a soldier. He returned to America in 1773 as a Lieutenant-Colonel on half-pay, frustrated in his attempts to gain further promotion. A follower of Rousseau, widely travelled and well-read, he became a fervent supporter of the American cause, and well known to many American leaders. In June 1775 he was made a Major-General, and resigned his British commission. He was popular and able to arouse enthusiasm in others, but was also temperamental, arrogant and unsteady. He was betrayed to the British in December 1776, and only Washington's intervention prevented his being court-martialled as a deserter. While a British prisoner, he was used as an intermediary in peace negotiations, and was later suspected by the Americans of having betrayed them. Alleged misconduct at and after Monmouth Court House led to his court-martial, and his suspension and dismissal from the army.

Cresswell found him in 1777 'a tall thin ill-looking man . . . about 50 years of age . . . very sensible, but rash and violent in his sentiments as well as actions'.

**102 Eighteenth century British weapons**

[*a*] Flintlock pistol for Light Dragoons 1765–70.

The pattern of this English pistol dates from 1759 when full regiments of Light Dragoons were authorized for the first time. This pistol, weighing about 2 lbs, remained the principal handgun of the dragoons during the American War of Independence. The lockplate is stamped 'Tower'.

*Lent by HM Tower of London, Armouries Inventory Number XII 819*

[*b*] British Light Dragoon sword, *c.* 1777–88

The simple brass hilt is of stirrup form, apparently the final stage in the development of British horseman blades before the War. The blade is back-edged, slightly curved and terminates in a clipped point.

*Lent by HM Tower of London, Armouries Inventory Number IX 1294*

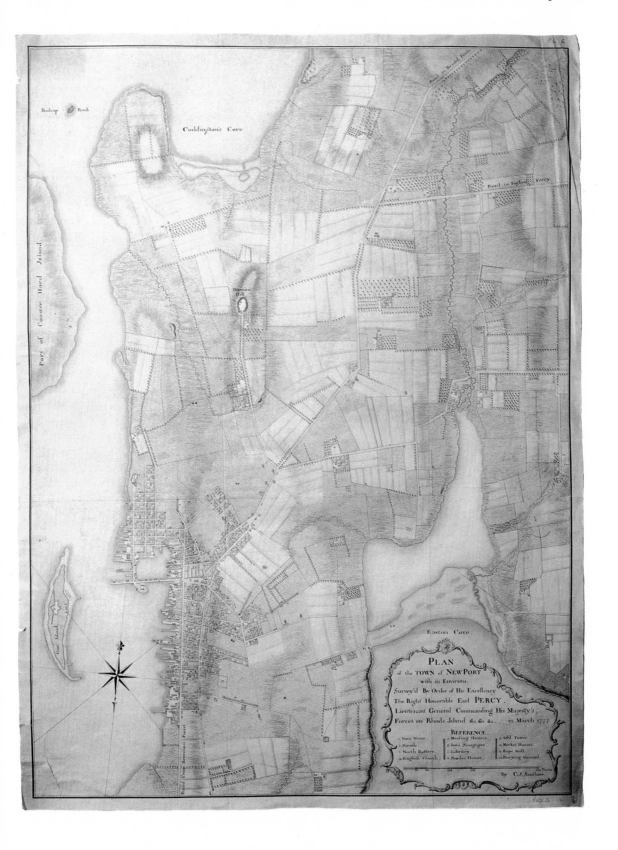

*Light Infantry Man and Huzzar of the Queen's Rangers.*

copied from a Drawing by Capt. Murray of the Queen's Rangers.

149

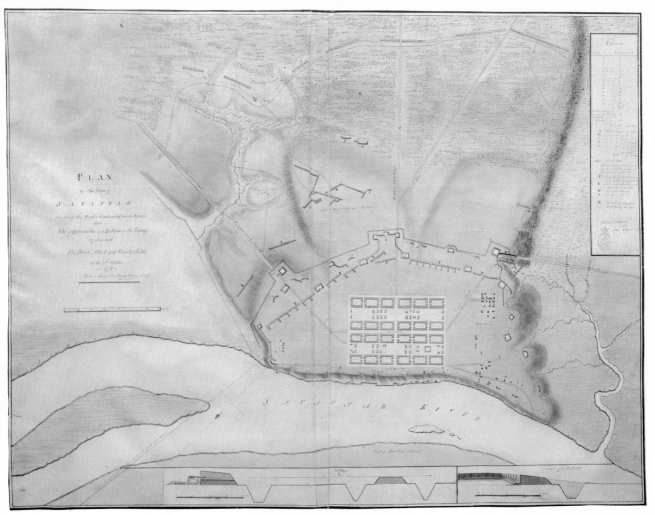

134

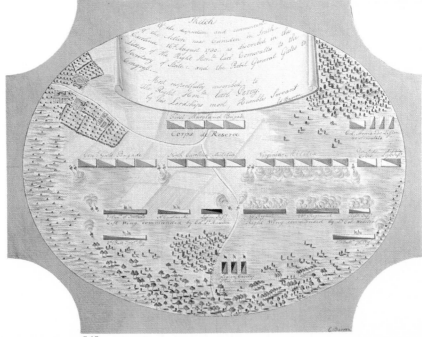

141

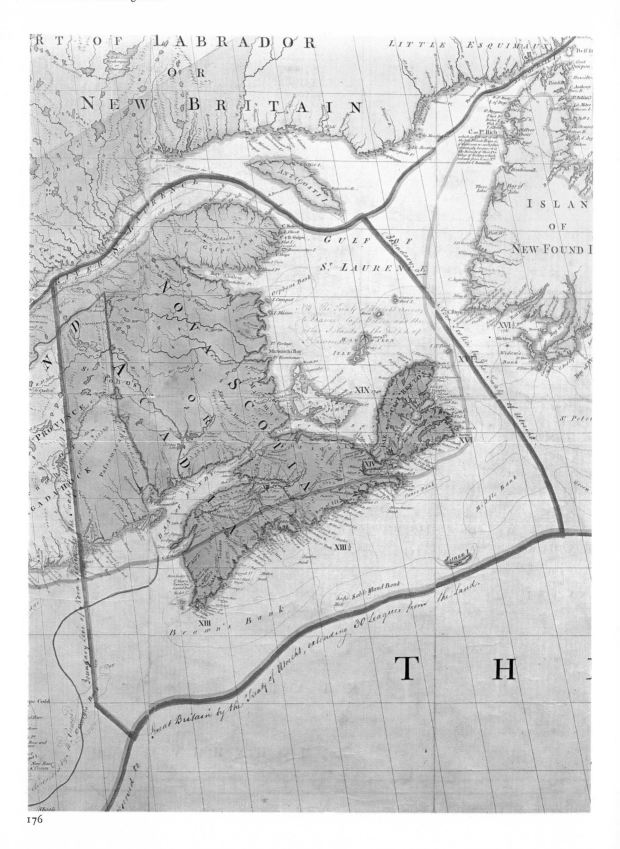

176

## 103 New York on the Eve of its Occupation

Plan of the City of New York in North
America: Surveyed in the years 1766 & 1767.
By B. Ratzer; A South West View of the City
of New York, taken from Governour's Island.
London, [*c*.1770].

1:100,000. 89 × 61cm

*BL Map Library K. Top. CXXI.36b*

Described by Stokes and Haskell in *American
Historical Prints* (1933) as: 'One of the most
beautiful, important, and accurate early maps of
New York' the Ratzer Map is based on an early
Ratzer plan, called the 'Ratzen Plan,' after an
engraving error, and published in 1769. The
'view' is an accurate depiction of New York in
the years 1767–70, indicating clearly the city sky-
line with its churches and chapels, and the prosperous harbour and shipyards. On the left of the
'view' are part of the Brooklyn Heights, so
important for the defence of the city, and Long
Island. The map depicts places later destroyed in
the fire of 1776, and Paulus Hook, whence the
incendiaries operated, according to one story.
At one time it was believed that the column of
smoke depicted in the view, represented the
Fire at New York, and was a later addition to
the map, but the smoke has been traced to a tar-
kettle on a small fire on the shore, where a ship
is undergoing repairs.

104

## 104 George Washington

Pastel portrait of George Washington
(1732–99), by Ellen Sharples after J. Sharples.

22 × 16cm

*Lent by the National Portrait Gallery*

Washington's achievement in raising and keep-
ing together the Continental Army, despite
several reverses, in this first period of the War,
when he himself was developing the qualities of
an effective commander-in-chief, was one of his
greatest services to his countrymen. This and
his tactical skill won him respect among his
opponents. Nicholas Cresswell believed him to
be 'one of Nature's geniuses, a Heaven-born
General, if there is any of that sort.' 'That a
Negro-driver should, with a ragged Banditti of
undisciplined people, the scum and refuse of all
nations on earth, so long keep a British General
at bay, nay, even oblige him, with as fine an
army of Veteran Soldiers as ever England had
on the American Continent . . . is astonishing'.

As an experienced general at the head of
seasoned troops and furnished with men and
supplies from abroad, Washington promised to
be an even greater menace to the British.

The RIGHT HON.ᴮᴸᴱ RICHARD LORD HOWE.
*Commander in Chief of his Majesty's Fleets in America.*

105

## 105 Admiral Lord Howe

Portrait of the Right Hon.ᵇˡᵉ Richard Lord Howe Commander-in-Chief of his Majesty's Fleets in America. Corbutt delin. London: John Morris, 1778.

Mezzotint. 33 × 24cm

*BM Department of Prints and Drawings*
1902-10-11-7073

Richard Lord Howe (1726–99) was appointed either through the patronage of Lord George Germain or as a conciliatory gesture by the Government to compensate him for failing to obtain a sinecure post that he coveted. He was well disposed towards the Americans and was a friend of Benjamin Franklin; this did not prevent the failure of his mission in 1776 as a peace commissioner. He was an experienced sailor but had little knowledge of the American situation. He was criticized for not being forceful enough in harrying the rebels. A taciturn man, 'unfeeling in his nature ... and ungracious in his manner', and disappointed at being made subordinate to the Earl of Carlisle in the Peace Commission of 1778, Howe returned to England, to join his brother in Parliament. He was later made First Lord of the Admiralty, and served with distinction in the Napoleonic Wars.

## 106 An oval medallion of Richard Earl Howe (1726–99). Bust in profile facing right on lilac ground. Impressed mark on back: WEDGWOOD. Modelled by John de Vaere, 1798

Height 3⅞in, 10cm

*BM Department of Medieval and Later Antiquities, Pottery Catalogue I. 54*

## 107 General Sir William Howe

Portrait of the Hon^ble Sr Wm Howe . . .

Commander in Chief of His Majesty's Forces in America. Corbutt delin.t et fecit. London: John Morris, 1777.

Mezzotint. 32 × 25 cm

*BM Department of Prints and Drawings* 1899-7-13-60

Sir William Howe (1729–1814) was a courageous and experienced soldier, who had led the assault on the Heights of Abraham, before Quebec, in the Seven Years' War. He had opposed the Government's American policy more strongly than his brother, but like him was made joint Commander-in-Chief and a peace commissioner, and in the interest of British trade, genuinely sought to bring about a favourable peace. After evacuating Boston, he directed the middle colonies operations with considerable success, but he proved too cautious, too slow, and too traditional in his military tactics to exploit his victories and destroy Washington's army. Most conspicuous was his failure to attack Washington in Valley Forge in 1777. He became increasingly aware of the enormity of his task and of his inadequacy as a leader. Too fond of comfort and too attentive to his mistresses, Howe lost popularity with his men. Pessimistic, wrongly believing that his wishes had been neglected by Germain, Howe resigned soon after Saratoga, to join the enemies of the Government in Parliament. He was a typical example of the soldiers and politicians on the British side; brave, fairly competent, incapable of understanding American feelings, and only slowly changing his policies and tactics to suit American conditions.

The HON^BLE Sr Wm HOWE.

Knight of the Bath, & Commander in Chief of his Majesty's Forces in America.

LONDON: Publish'd as the Act directs, 10th Nov.r 1777 by JOHN MORRIS, Rathbone Place.

107

A HESSIAN GRENADEIR

108

## 108 Hessian mercenaries

'A Hessian Grenadeir'. London: M. Darley,
1 August 1778.

23 × 16cm

*BM Department of Prints and Drawings, Satires*
*5483*

The grenadier wears the typical long pigtail,
short shaggy hair, pointed metal mitre-shaped
hat, coat and jack-boots. Among the items on
his back are a flask, a pouch, a goose or turkey,
and a leg of mutton. He holds a musket with a
fixed bayonet.

Hessians formed the greater part of the German
mercenaries employed by the British in America.
They were essential to the British cause; on occasions they proved brave and valiant soldiers,
and had capable men among their officers, such
as Knyphausen. The British, however, had re-
servations about using them. Their habit of
plundering friend and foe alike antagonized
both rebels and Loyalists. Americans feared and
detested them as foreign mercenaries, and British officers complained that the large quantities
of baggage they carried slowed them down.
Nicholas Cresswell thought them, 'fine troops,
but very slow in their motions when compared
with the English'. Their heavy clothing and
boots appeared unsuited to the American summer. After their conduct at Trenton, their reputation fell still further. Ambrose Serle, Lord
Howe's secretary, stated in a passage later dele-
ted from his journal: 'It is a misfortune, we
ever had such a dirty, cowardly set of contemptible miscreants.'

## 109 The North River Expedition

Captain Hyde Parker in the Phoenix going up
the North River, New York, 1776.
Watercolour by Dominic Serres.

29 × 48cm

*BM Department of Prints and Drawings*
1879-8-9-655

Parker's ship the *Phoenix*, and the *Rose*, captain-
ed by James Wallace, are depicted in this watercolour. On 12 July 1776 'about noon the Phoenix of forty guns and the Rose of twenty, with
three Tenders forced their Passage up the
North [or Hudson] River in Defiance of all
their vaunted Batteries, and [are] safe above the
Town [New York], which will much intercept
the Provisions of the Rebels'. Lord Howe planned this mission to disrupt rebel communications across the Hudson, and to keep the river
open for General Burgoyne, supposedly advancing south from Albany. The ships braved
American gunboats, fireships, batteries and
*chevaux de frise* (man-made barriers) to cut rebel
supplies and inflict casualties with little loss,
before rejoining Howe 'with sails set and colours flying' on 18 August for the assault on
Long Island. This exploit, which 'much dis-
heartened' the rebels and raised British morale,
earned both captains knighthoods.

For Colour Plate, see p. 20

GEORGE WASHINGTON, Esq.ʳ

GENERAL and COMMANDER in CHIEF of the CONTINENTAL ARMY in AMERICA.

61

Image caption text: SIR HYDE PARKER CAPTAIN of the PHOENIX.

110

## 110 Portrait of Captain Hyde Parker

Portrait of Captain Hyde Parker of the *Phoenix*.
Engraving by James Walker after a painting
by George Romney. London, J. Walker,
1 June 1780.

67 × 39cm

*BM Department of Prints and Drawings*
1902-10-11-6098.

Hyde Parker (1739–1807) ended his long career
as Admiral Sir Hyde Parker, in command of the
British assault on Copenhagen in 1801. His
reputation was then sullied by his over-cautious
handling of the attack. Nelson was to turn his
blind eye to Parker's signals to break off the
engagement. Twenty-five years earlier, however, Parker showed considerable courage and
determination in his leading of the North River
expedition. He was rewarded with a knight-

hood, and was to see further action off New
York and Rhode Island, on the Savannah expedition of 1779, in the North Atlantic, and at
the relief of Gibraltar.

## 111 The Battle of Long Island, 1776

A Plan of New York Island, with part of Long
Island, Staten Island & East New Jersey, with
a particular Description of the Engagement on
the Woody Heights of Long Island between
Flatbush and Brooklyn on the 27th of August
1776. London: Wᵐ Faden, Oct 19th 1776.

1:85,000. 49 × 43cm

*BL Map Library* 73956.(3)

The Howes arrived off New York just after the
Declaration of Independence and the destruction of the royal statue; their subsequent attempts to overawe the colonists or to start
negotiations inevitably failed. General Howe,
now joined by Clinton, landed 20,000 men unopposed on Long Island. Washington faced him
with 9,000 men of uncertain quality; their inexperienced leader had erred in sending a further division into a potentially dangerous position and now failed to spot that the American
left flank ended in open country guarded by
only five men. Howe, at Clinton's suggestion,
engaged the American centre and right while
skilfully outflanking them on their left. Only
Lord Stirling on the right offered prolonged
resistance, and soon the Americans were fleeing
in confusion to their Brooklyn entrenchments.

General Howe now erred in preparing for a
lengthy siege instead of overrunning the
American entrenchments. Admiral Howe, in-
tending to entrap Washington by occupying
the East River, was forestalled by contrary
winds, and on 29 August Washington ferried his
men to Manhattan at night in a thick fog. This
remarkable escape did not dishearten his opponents. The British were 'so close to New York
that you could see people walking in the streets
and even distinguish the color of their clothes'.
Lord Percy expressed the general view that
'this business is pretty near over'.

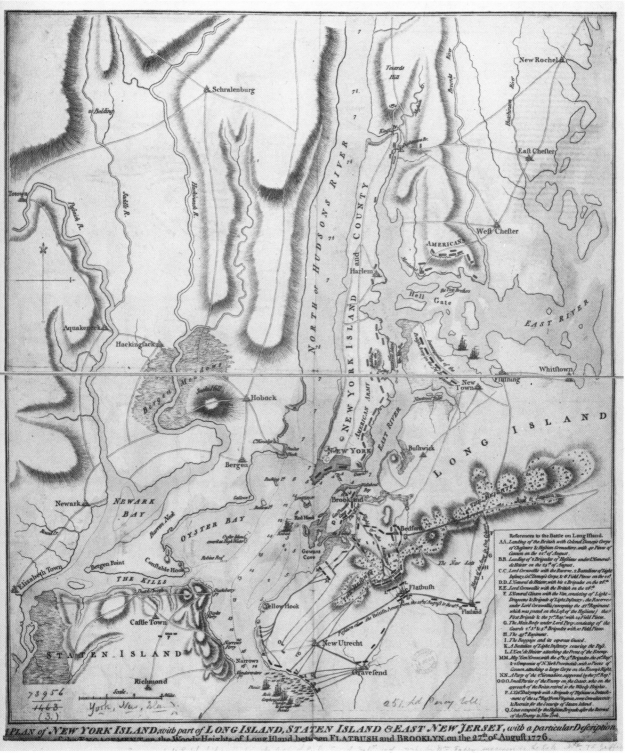

A PLAN of *NEW YORK ISLAND*, with part of *LONG ISLAND, STATEN ISLAND & EAST NEW JERSEY*, with a particular Description of the ENGAGEMENT on the Woody Heights of Long Island between FLATBUSH and BROOKLYN, on the 27th of August 1776.

References to the Battle on Long Island.

AA. *Landing of the British with Colonel Donops Corps of Chasseurs & Hessian Grenadiers, with 40 Pieces of Cannon on the 22d of August.*
BB. *Landing of 2 Brigades of Hessians under L.l General de Heister on the 25.th of August.*
CC. *Lord Cornwallis with the Reserve, 2 Battalions of Light Infantry, Col.l Donop's Corp, & 6 Field Piece on the 21.st*
DD. *L.l General de Heister with his 2 Brigades on the 26.th*
EE. *Lord Cornwallis with the British on the 26.th*
Y.Y. *L.l General Clinton with the Van, consisting of Light Dragoons & Brigade of Light Infantry, the Reserve under Lord Cornwallis, excepting the 42 Regiment which was posted on the Left of the Hessians, the First Brigade & the 71.st Reg.t with 14 Field Piece.*
G. *The Main Body under Lord Percy, consisting of the Guards & 2.d & 3.d Brigades with 10 Field Piece.*
H. *The 42.d Regiment.*
I. *The Baggage and its separate Guard.*
K. *A Battalion of Light Infantry securing the Pass.*
L. *L.t Gen.l de Heister attacking the Front of the Enemy.*
MM. *Maj Gen.l Grant with the 4.th & 6.th Brigades, the 2.d Reg.t & 2 Companies of N. York Provincials with 10 Pieces of Cannon, attacking a large Corps on the Enemy's Right.*
NN. *A Party of the 2.d Grenadiers, supposed by the 71.st Reg.t*
OOO. *Small Parties of the Enemy on the Coast, who on the approach of the Boats retired to the Woody Heights.*
P. *L.t Col.l Dalrymple with a Brigade of Highlanders & Detachments of the 24 Reg.t from Virginia, some Convalescents & Recruits for the Security of Staten Island.*
Q. *Lines occupied by the Hessian Brigade after the Retreat of the Enemy to New York.*

Scale

Miles

*Collection des Prospects.* L'ENTRÉE TRIUMPHALE DE TROUPES ROYALES A NOUVELLE YORCK.

*Gravé par François Xav. Habermann*

*Der Einzug der Königlichen Völcker in Neu Yorck.* | *L'Entré triumphale de Troupes royales a Nouvelle Yorck.*

113

**112** An account of the Battle of Long Island; a graphic account of the end of the fighting.

*MS unsigned.* 30 × 20cm

*BL Department of Manuscripts Egerton MS* 2135, *f.*193

'A general Confusion ensued on the part of the rebels & they were defeated & routed with great Slaughter – They fled on all sides & were cut to pieces in their retreat by the third column who came up with them just as they were getting into their redoubts. . .' There were only about 8,000 rebels involved in the fighting, not 40,000 as the writer states; the number of rebel casualties is also exaggerated. The British captured '6 Brass Field Pieces – 1 Brass Howitzer inscribed United Colonies – 5 Stand of Regimental Colours & a great number of Iron Ordnance,

Artillery Stores and Provisions'. Some American troops were fighting on the British side, for the writer adds that 'The New York Vol-[untee]rs took 2 Field Pieces'.

## 113 The British Enter New York, 1776

L'Entré triumphale du Troupes royales a Nouvelle Yorck. Gravé par François Xav. Habermann, Augsbourg [*c.*1776].

28 × 40cm

*BM Department of Prints and Drawings* 1898-7-25-8 (1295)

The British soldiers marched into New York in September 1776, after Howe's successful landing to the north at Kips Bay. They are depicted marching in columns to the sound of drum and fife, through streets largely deserted save for a

*Collection des Prospects*

*Schröckenvolle Feuersbrunst welche zu Neu York von deren Americanern in der Nacht vom 19. Herbst Monath 1776. angeleget worden, wodurch alle Gebäude auf der West Seite der neuen Börse, längst der Broockstrent bis an das König Kollegii mehr als 1600. Häuser, die Dreyfaltigkeits Kirche, die Lutherische Kappelle u. die armen Schule in Asche verwandelt worden.*

*Représentation du Feu terrible a Nouvelle Vorck, que les Americains ont allume pendent la Nuit du 19. Septembre 1776. par le quel ont été brulés, tous les Batiments du Côté de l'est, a droite de Börse dans la Rue de Broock jusqu'au Collége du Roi et plus que 1600. Maisons avec L'Eglise de la S.te Trinité la Chapelle Lutheriche et L'Ecole des pauvres*

114

few anxious onlookers. Some British observers stated that the troops received a rapturous welcome, but the engraver follows other authorities, such as the Howes themselves, who found their reception and the support given them disappointing.

## 114 The Fire at New York

Representation du Feu terrible a Nouvelle Yorck. Gravé par François Xav. Habermann. Augsbourg, [*c*.1776].

28 × 40cm

*BM Department of Prints and Drawings*
1898-7-25-8

The British had suspected that the Americans would burn New York, to reduce its value to them. After the British occupied it on the fifteenth, a fire broke out on 19–20 September which destroyed from a quarter to a third of the city, including a Lutheran Chapel and Holy Trinity Church, and property of considerable value. The engraving depicts a street in flames, with servants and slaves rescuing property from the blaze. Soldiers threaten a captured incendiary and his companions who are caught damaging or overturning some fire-buckets. Figures in the background are probably conspirators running away. Some arsonists who were caught were thrown into the flames or stabbed and hung from posts. The fire also served to delay a projected attack on Paulus Hook. The city was to remain partly in ruins, half-deserted and rife with disease, for the rest of the War, another fire breaking out in the dockland in 1778. The fire of 1776 was possibly an accident, but Washington, Howe and others believed that Patriots were involved.

### 115 New York After the Fire

Plan of the City of New York as it was when His Majesty's Forces took possession of it in 1776 . . . Survey'd in October 1776 by C. J. Sauthier.

MS 1:5376 approx. 80 × 59cm

*Lent by His Grace the Duke of Northumberland*

Sauthier's plan covers roughly the same area as the Ratzer map but also indicates the fortifications prepared by the Americans and the area affected by the recent great fire.

### 116 The Capture of Forts Washington and Lee, 1776

A Topographical Map of the North.<sup>n</sup> part of New York Island, Exhibiting the Plan of Fort Washington, now Fort Knyphausen, with the Rebels Lines to the Southward, which were Forced by the Troops under . . . Earl Percy on the 16th November 1776 . . . By Claude Joseph Sauthier.

London: W.<sup>m</sup> Faden, March 1st 1777.

1:21,000 approx. 26 × 47cm

*BL Map Library 73956. (4)*

Forts Washington and Lee were originally part of Washington's defence of his communications between New Jersey and Connecticut via the lower Hudson. Fort Washington was considered impregnable. Washington considered abandoning it when Howe's movements after White Plains forced him to disperse his forces to cover all the possible lines of attack, but wrongly deferred to General Greene and the garrison commander. General Knyphausen and Lord Percy stormed the outer defences and forced the garrison to submit. Prisoners numbering 2,900 and large quantities of arms and supplies were taken. Fort Lee was hastily abandoned, and later occupied by Cornwallis. This was for the Americans another severe, and avoidable, disaster.

Trained in Strasbourg as an architect and surveyor, Sauthier (1736–1802) had served Governor Tryon in North Carolina and New York (1767–75), and with the outbreak of war was now employed by Lord Percy as military surveyor.

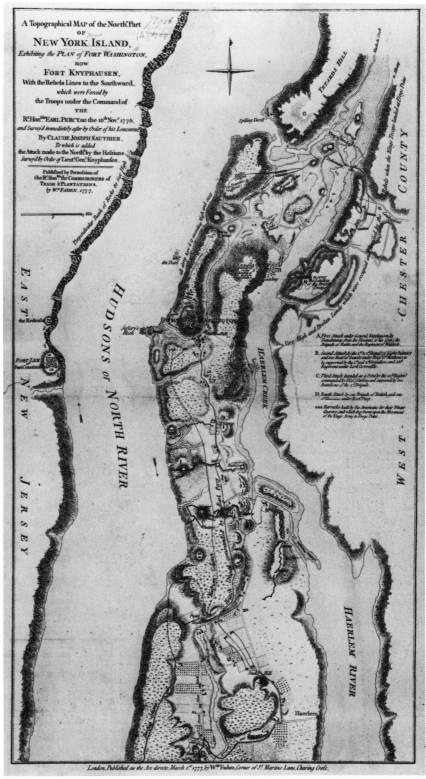

*News from America, or the Patriots in the Dumps.*

Willces.                    Mansfield. North  Bute    Geo.3.
                                              I.R Sandwich

117

## 117 'News from America, or the Patriots in the Dumps', 1776

Cartoon engraved in the *London Magazine* November 1776.

16 × 11cm

*BM Department of Prints and Drawings* 1868-8-8-10077

While British men of war sink American vessels in the background, the Prime Minister, Lord North, and Lord Mansfield, the Lord Chief Justice stand on a platform, the former holding aloft a dispatch from Lord Howe reporting further British successes before a des-pondent audience of patriots, including John Wilkes. A weeping woman bears the cap of liberty balanced on a smoking-pipe. Behind North stand the King and Lord Bute, once his favourite and adviser; in front of the King is Lord Sandwich, a 'List of the Navy' hanging from his pocket, and another minister nearby, possibly Germain, is amused at the patriots' despair.

This engraving, at first sight the work of a Loyalist, in fact accompanies an article written to show that ministerial optimism was misplaced and illusory, being only 'the beginning of sorrows'.

## 118 The Battle of White Plains, 1776

A Plan of the operations of the King's Army under the Command of General Sir William Howe . . . in New York and East New Jersey . . . from the 12th of October to the 28th of November 1776, wherein is particularly distinguished the Engagement on the White Plain the 28th of October. By Claude Joseph Sauthier. Engraved by W. Faden 1777. London: Wᵐ. Faden, 25 Feb. 1777

1:90,000. 49 × 73cm

*BL Map Library 1. TAB. 44. (24)*

The operations were intended to force Washington to meet Howe's army in the open, by threatening his links with the mainland. Washington was forced out of Manhattan and New Jersey; his garrison at Fort Washington surrendered, and Fort Lee was abandoned. American morale was low; militiamen failed to turn out; Philadelphia was deserted by Congress and many of its inhabitants; yet Howe failed to destroy the Continental Army. His best opportunity was at White Plains, where Washington offered battle to protect his Lower Hudson communications. Howe failed to follow up his seizure of a strategically important hill and his planned assault was delayed by rain, while Washington slipped away to a stronger position. The operation ended with Washingtons'

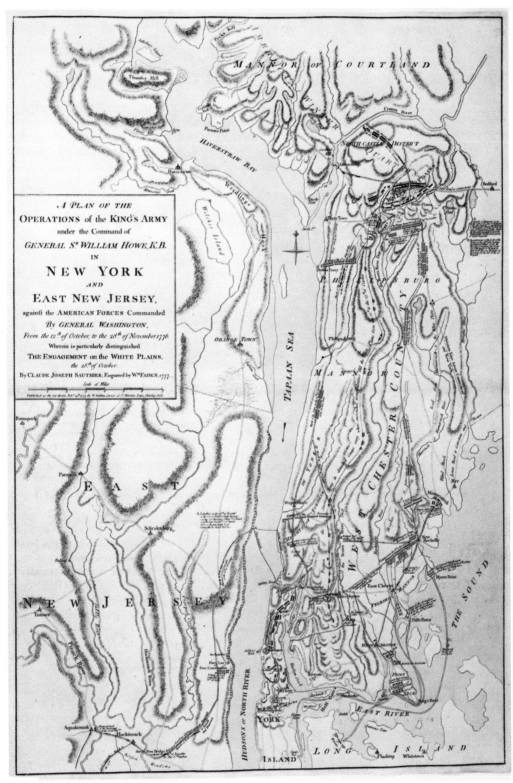

A PLAN OF THE
OPERATIONS of the KING'S ARMY
under the Command of
GENERAL Sr. WILLIAM HOWE, K.B.
IN
NEW YORK
AND
EAST NEW JERSEY,
againſt the AMERICAN FORCES Commanded
By GENERAL WASHINGTON,
From the 12th of October, to the 28th of November 1776.
Wherein is particularly diſtinguiſhed
THE ENGAGEMENT on the WHITE PLAINS,
the 28th of October.
By CLAUDE JOSEPH SAUTHIER, Engraved by Wm. FADEN, 1777.

army still intact, and its leader planning counter-moves against scattered British outposts in West New Jersey from across the Delaware. On 30 November the Howes made their latest peace move, a general offer of pardon.

## 119 Newport

Plan of the Town of Newport with its Environs. Survey'd by order of His Excellency The Right Honorable Earl Percy, Lieutenant General Commanding His Majesty's Forces on Rhode Island . . . March 1777. By C. J. Sauthier.

MS 1:6144 approx. 73 × 97cm

*Lent by His Grace the Duke of Northumberland*

This topographical map is a fine example of Sauthier's work as a military surveyor. When Lord Percy returned to England in May 1777 he took Sauthier with him as his private secretary, and on succeeding as second Duke of Northumberland, employed him as estate surveyor. For Colour Plate, see p. 93

## 120 Trenton and Princeton, 1776–7

Plan of the Operations of General Washington, against the King's Troops in New Jersey, from the 26th of December 1776, to the 3rd January 1777. Wm Faden, 1777.

1:115,000 approx. 40 × 30cm

*BL Map Library* 73845.(2)

These two victories were possibly Washington's finest, at a time when he felt the cause desperate. Unless he obtained more men, he said 'I think the game will be pretty well up'. He had to counter-attack to lessen the effect of Howe's proclamation, and to keep alive the rebel cause in New Jersey, before the New Year when his army would be disbanded. Three detachments were to attack Trenton and Bordentown and drive on, if possible, to Princeton and New Brunswick. Two failed to cross the Delaware but Washington took 2,400 men through snow, storm and river ice to catch Colonel Rall's

1,400 Hessians off-guard after their Christmas celebrations at Trenton. Thirty Hessians died, including Rall, and 918 were captured; the rest fled to Bordentown. The commanding officer at Bordentown retreated precipitately without orders, making matters worse. Cornwallis pressed Washington hard, believing that he had 'bagged the fox', but the latter crept away at night, struck a sharp blow at a weak royal force at Princeton, and escaped to a highland winter stronghold at Morristown.

Howe now abandoned all New Jersey except for a bridgehead. He found 'The Rebels have taken fresh courage upon this event . . .', Robert Morris at Philadelphia reported, 'the Militia of this place, Maryland & Jersey begin to turn out and think themselves good soldiers. . . . the spirit of the Whigs is up, and the Tories hide their heads.'

## 121 Ministers React to Trenton, 1777

Letter from Lord George Germain to William Eden concerning the disaster at Trenton, 25 February 1777.

MS, autograph.

*BL Department of Manuscripts Add. MS* 34413, f.267

Three weeks earlier Germain had been jubilant concerning the British successes: 'The military operations have ended as gloriously as could be expected. . . . I think Sir William Howe has shown great knowledge in his Profession.' Now news of Trenton had reached Britain, and Ministers were aware of its implications, as Germain wrote, 'you see the business of the Hessian defeat in its true light; the loss is not considerable but I fear the consequences both in France and in America'.

All hope of an imminent American collapse had gone and Britain with her resources already overstretched now faced a resurgent Congress and the likelihood of French intervention in the New World and the Old.

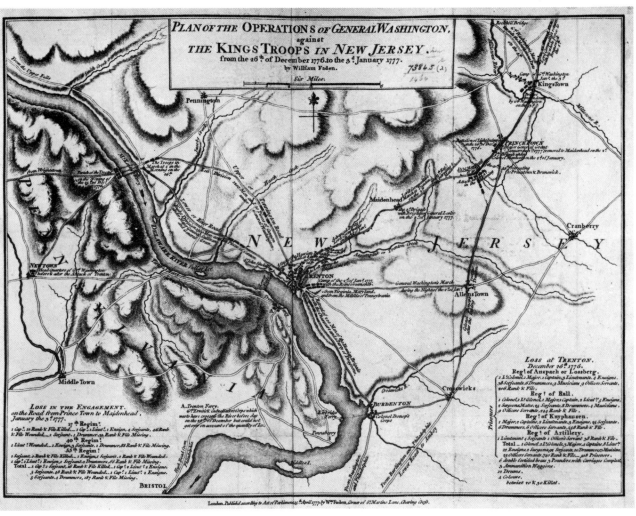

## 122 Criticism of the Howe Brothers

Letter from George III to John Robinson, 5 March 1777.

MS, autograph. 22 × 18cm

*BL Department of Manuscripts*
*Add. MS 37833, f.137*

The King was still confident after Trenton, believing that if the Howes 'will act with a little less lenity (which I really think cruelty, as it keeps up the contest) the next campaign will bring the Americans in a temper to accept of such terms as may enable the mother country to keep them in order... the regaining their affection is an idle idea, it must be the convincing them that it is their interest to submit, and then they will dread further broils'.

Criticism of the brothers' lenity towards the rebels and their casual conduct of affairs mounted during 1777. As peace commissioners they had attempted to avoid antagonizing their opponents and had tried to win back American support by persuasion rather than by force. No tight blockade of American ports was attempted and they were reluctant to approve raids on rebel harbours and supply depots. They were also considered too liberal in issuing pardons to rebels, many of whom defected after the battle at Trenton. Some of the blame for the Howes' ambivalent attitude to their military duties must rest with the Government who decided to make them both commanders-in-chief and peace commissioners. The King here rejects General Howe's request for 20,000 more men as 'impracticable'. Britain had insufficient troops to meet such a demand. Howe was later to complain, unfairly, that his requests had been ignored by the Government.

The 'Mr Galloway' referred to was probably Joseph Galloway, who joined Howe's army in December 1776. He was later to be a fierce critic of the Howes' conduct of the War.

## 123 Brandywine Creek

Battle of Brandywine, in which the Rebels were defeated, September 11th 1777, by the Army under the command of General S.<sup>r</sup> Will.<sup>m</sup> Howe. Engraved by W.<sup>m</sup> Faden, London: W.<sup>m</sup> Faden, 1778.

1:16,000 approx. 58 × 48cm

*BL Map Library* 74950. (4)

Howe sailed from New York with 13,000 men on 23 July 1777 and landed at Head of Elk on Chesapeake Bay on 25 August en route for Philadelphia. A delayed start, and the diversion of the fleet from Delaware Bay, on Howe being informed incorrectly that Washington was advancing to meet him there, made any later movements to help Burgoyne impossible. Washington now confidently expected 'the total ruin of Burgoyne' and posted his 11,000 men on the north side of Brandywine Creek, to await Howe's approach. Howe's army, tired, denied provisions and harassed by the Americans, was again victorious. Knyphausen launched a diversionary frontal attack, while Cornwallis marched westwards, crossed the river and fell on the badly protected American right flank under Sullivan. Washington wisely forebore to press Knyphausen, and sent Greene's division to cover Sullivan's escape. Greene accomplished this, and successfully covered Washington's retreat before Knyphausen's attack. The retreat soon became a rout, and only nightfall and Howe's lack of an adequate cavalry force prevented an overwhelming defeat. Washington's casualties were again twice those of Howe's, but he was able, unlike the latter, to recoup his losses. Howe took Philadelphia, but Burgoyne was left to his fate without adequate support.

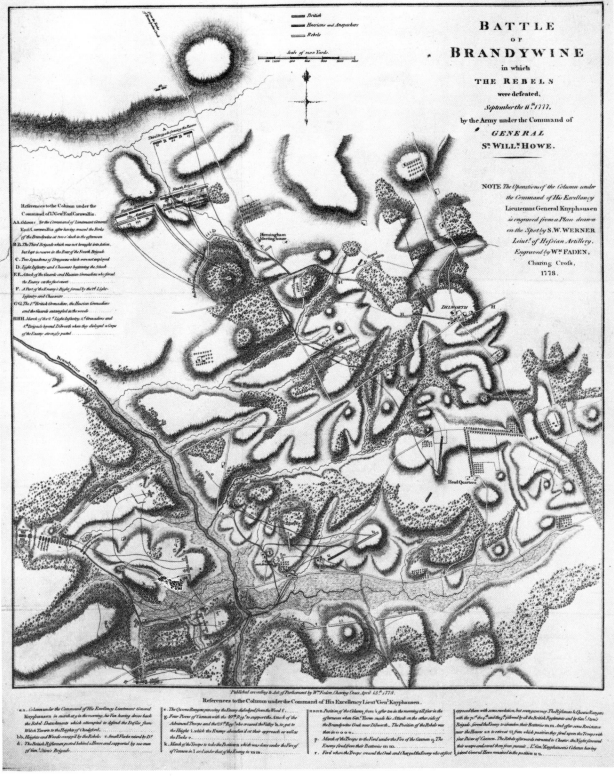

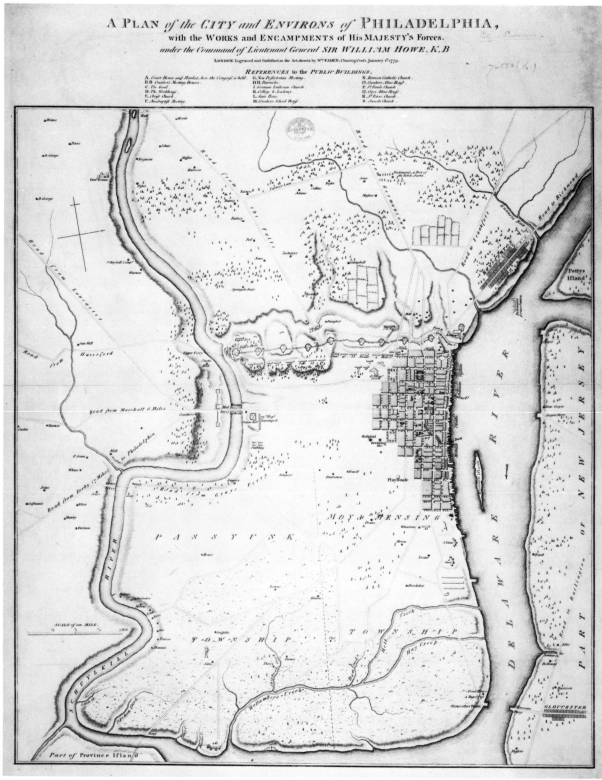

## 124 The British Occupation of Philadelphia

A Plan of the City and Environs of Philadelphia, with the works and encampments of His Majesty's Forces under the command of . . . Sir William Howe. London: W$^m$. Faden, 1779.

1:21,000 approx. 56 × 47cm

*BL. Map Library* 74580.(16)

The plan shows the main British encampment on an upland edge extending from the Schuykill to the Delaware, to the north of the city, and defence works at the bridge of boats over the Schuykill, at the ferries, on the Delaware to the south of the city and on the river banks. Men of war are depicted moored in the Delaware.

Cresswell found the Quaker City in 1776 'the most regular, neat and convenient city I ever was in', well set out with wide streets and 'neat plain buildings'; its State House was until the British occupation 'the nest of the great and mighty Sanhedrim', or the meeting place of the American Congress.

## 125 Surprise at Germantown

Sketch of the Surprise of German Town by the American Forces commanded by General Washington October 4th 1777.
By J. Hills. London: W$^m$. Faden, March 12th 1784.

1:23,500 approx. 50 × 65cm

*BL Map Library RUSI A30/6.*

At Germantown Washington attempted to repeat his success at Trenton. Eleven thousand Americans engaged 9,000 British troops in a surprise early morning attack. Howe, not expecting an attack on a potentially strong position, had made no entrenchments and had provided only a weak advance guard. Washington intended to assault the enemy flanks and rear, while a two-column frontal attack captured the town and split the enemy in two. The rear and right flank attacks were tardily delivered and were repulsed; but Washington, though detected, drove the British advance guard back, until held by Colonel Musgrave and men of the 40th Foot. Time was wasted in trying to dislodge him, and Knyphausen was able to form a defence line in the town. The British and Hessians were hard-pressed, however, until a thick fog, their resistance, and Musgrave's fire created confusion among the colonials. Cornwallis's arrival with reinforcements turned a retreat into flight. The Americans suffered twice as many casualties as the British, but had fought well, and claimed a moral victory. News of Saratoga further heartened the patriots, while Howe abandoned his post, resigning the next year. His worst failure was to neglect to follow up Washington's poor choice of winter quarters, allowing the Continental Army to freeze unmolested in Valley Forge.

126

126 An English medal commemorating the occupation of Chew's House at Shippock Creek by Troops of the 40th Regiment under Lt. Col. Musgrave during the Battle of Germantown. Engraved by John Milton, assistant at the Royal Mint 1789–98, whose works date from 1760.

45mm diam.

*BM Department of Coins and Medals Betts 556*

Chew's House was built about 1761 by Benjamin Chew, Chief Justice of Pennsylvania 1774–77, who was imprisoned as a loyalist in 1777. Musgrave played a valuable role in this battle by placing part of his regiment, the 40th Foot, in the house and thus causing the Americans to waste about an hour and a half in attempting to dislodge him. The *Annual Register* for 1777 recorded that: 'The Colonel and his brave party, surrounded by a whole Brigade and attacked on every side with great resolution, defended the house with the most undaunted courage; and though the enemy at length brought Cannon up to the assault, he still maintained his post with equal Intrepidity pouring a dreadful and unceasing fire through the windows until affairs had taken such a turn as afforded him relief.'

### 127 Forts Clinton and Montgomery

Plan of the Attack of the Forts Clinton & Montgomery upon Hudsons River which were Stormed by His Majesty's Forces under Sir Henry Clinton . . . 6th of Oct$^r$, 1777, by J. Hills. London: W$^m$ Faden 1784.

1:21,500 approx. 55 × 70cm

*BL Map Library* 74190.(121)

The plan indicates the bold nature of Sir Henry Clinton's assault on these forts. He led his small force twelve miles through hilly hostile territory long closed to royal forces. The attack was planned as a diversion to help Burgoyne's increasingly difficult journey south. Clinton was fortunate in that Putnam, the commanding officer in that sector, had been obliged to send many of his troops to other areas of conflict, and so withdrew on Clinton's approach to an inland-base, taking men from the forts. Marching without cannon, Clinton surprised and took the forts with the bayonet at daybreak. He wrote to Burgoyne: '*Nous y Voila*, and nothing now between us but Gates. I sincerely hope this little success may facilitate your operations . . .' Burgoyne never received the note; Clinton's messenger was caught and hanged. General Howe's requests for more troops for his invasion of Pennsylvania prevented further movement to the north, and these strategically valuable gains were abandoned shortly afterwards on his orders. Howe had left Clinton with insufficient forces for any major operation to help Burgoyne; both remained largely ignorant of his plight, until they received news of his surrender.

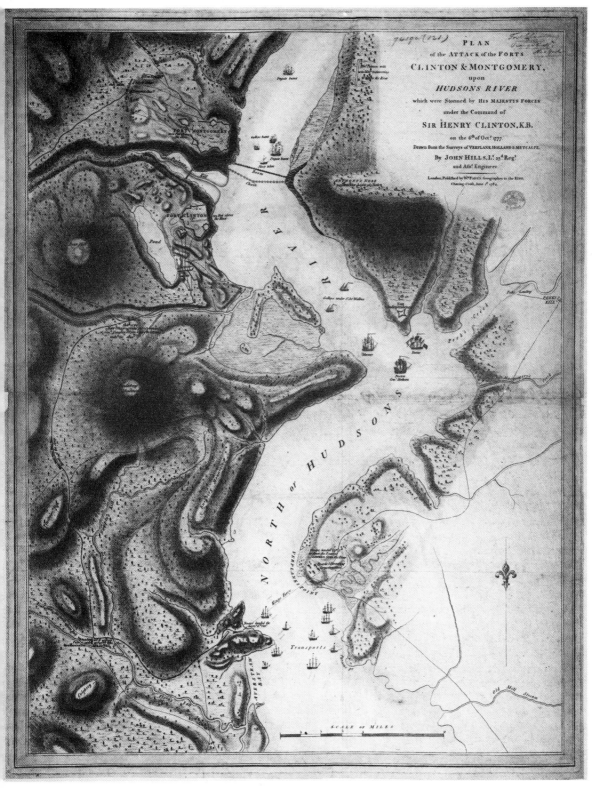

PLAN
of the ATTACK of the FORTS
CLINTON & MONTGOMERY,
upon
HUDSONS RIVER
which were Stormed by HIS MAJESTYS FORCES
under the Command of
SIR HENRY CLINTON, K.B.
on the 6th of Oct.r 1777.
Drawn from the Surveys of VERPLANK. HOLLAND & METCALFE.
By JOHN HILLS, L.t 25.d Reg.t
and Ass.t Engineer.

London, Published by Wm FADEN, Geographer to the KING.
Charing-Cross, June 1st 1784.

127

128

### 128 General Sir Henry Clinton (1738 ?–95)

Sir Henry Clinton. Miniature by John Smart, *c.*1777.

*Lent by the National Army Museum*

Having distinguished himself in the Battle of Bunker Hill in June 1775, Sir Henry Clinton was promoted to the rank of local General in 1776. He was also commissioned in the same year to act as second in command to General Sir William Howe, whom he eventually replaced as Commander-in-Chief of the forces in North America in early 1778. Clinton was thought by Charles Stuart, the Earl of Bute's son, to be unfit to command even a troop of horse. Dilatory, and frequently over-cautious, Clinton's temperament contrasted strongly with that of his immediate subordinate, Lord Cornwallis, an aggressive man who was intent on pursuing an offensive rather than a defensive war. Their mutual antagonism during the campaigns which were to follow in the south, culminated in bitter accusations which each published against the other following the final British surrender at Yorktown in 1781. Clinton resigned his post on 8 May 1782 and was succeeded by Sir Guy Carleton.

# V The War in the Southern Colonies 1778–81

The entry of France into the conflict following the Franco-American Treaty of February 1778 and the Alliance in May, caused Britain to reappraise her strategic policy. The ministers in London, assuming that there was a vast untapped reservoir of Loyalist strength in the south and that the royal fleet could maintain supremacy on the sea, suggested to Sir Henry Clinton that he dispatch troops to Georgia and attempt the conquest of the south. Although Sir William Howe had warned Lord George Germain that Britain could not rely on securing Tory help anywhere in America, the success of Lieut-Col. Campbell and General Prevost in re-establishing royal authority in Georgia in 1778 and 1779 opened the way for Clinton to proceed personally against Charleston, the capital of South Carolina. Following the fall of this city to the King's army, Clinton returned to New York leaving the south in the control of Lord Charles Cornwallis, who went on to win a resounding victory over General Gates at the battle of Camden in August 1780.

The destruction of two American Continental armies at Charleston and Camden temporarily paralysed Americans in the lower south, but the constant fierce raids of Lieut-Col. Banastre Tarleton, while harshly effective, spurred on the fainter hearted Patriots to participate in the conflict. Guerrilla warfare came to replace traditional fighting. Partisan officers like Thomas Sumter, Francis Marion and Colonel Andrew Pickets led their own groups of men, harassing the enemy at every opportunity and from every direction. Cornwallis's long-standing ambition to thrust northward and conquer Virginia was not initially approved by Clinton, who favoured the more cautious policy of consolidating British control in South Carolina followed by a gradual extension of royal possessions.

Allowed to take offensive action on condition that the safety of South Carolina was not endangered, Cornwallis adopted unorthodox methods in his pursuit of the Americans. The subsequent defeats of Ferguson at King's Mountain and Tarleton at Cowpens, the costly victory at Guildford Court House and the 'hit and run' tactics of the new southern commander, Nathanael Greene, combined to erode the strength of Cornwallis's army and the authority of His Majesty's Government in the south. He had failed to achieve the strategic aim of the southern campaign, which was to rally the Loyalists and maintain their support in order to effect the British occupation of the Carolinas. A disillusioned Cornwallis wrote to his superior; 'The weakness and treachery of our friends in South Carolina, and the impossibility of getting any military assistance from them, makes the possession of any part of the country of very little use.' Of the Patriots he wrote that the number of British soldiers dead and wounded 'proves but too fatally that they are not wholly contemptible.'

Confused by contradictory orders from Clinton and Germain, Cornwallis on his own initiative resolved to attempt the consolidation of British control in the South by the conquest of Virginia. The mutual antipathy between Cornwallis and the Commander-in-Chief led to disagreement on the strategic importance of Washington's own state. Clinton preferred to defend New York, and was only prepared to send small raiding parties to Virginia in. December 1780.

Learning of the British presence in the Old Dominion, Washington dispatched the French General, Lafayette, with three regiments of light infantry to defend the state. Cornwallis worsted his young opponent in several skirmishes, but finally instructed by Clinton 'to take up a defensive station in any healthy position he preferred', he retired to Yorktown and began constructing extensive fortifications in early August. The Franco-American forces, under Rochambeau and Washington moved swiftly south from New York and joined Lafayette in September. Over 15,000 allied troops now besieged the British army of 7,500 in Yorktown. The French Admiral de Grasse and his fleet had won the race with the British to Chesapeake Bay, defeating His Majesty's navy and forcing them to withdraw to New York.

The Allies commenced a thunderous artillery barrage on Yorktown on 9 October, but not until 17 October did Clinton send a fleet to relieve Cornwallis. By the time they arrived, Cornwallis, bereft of all expected reinforcements, had surrendered.

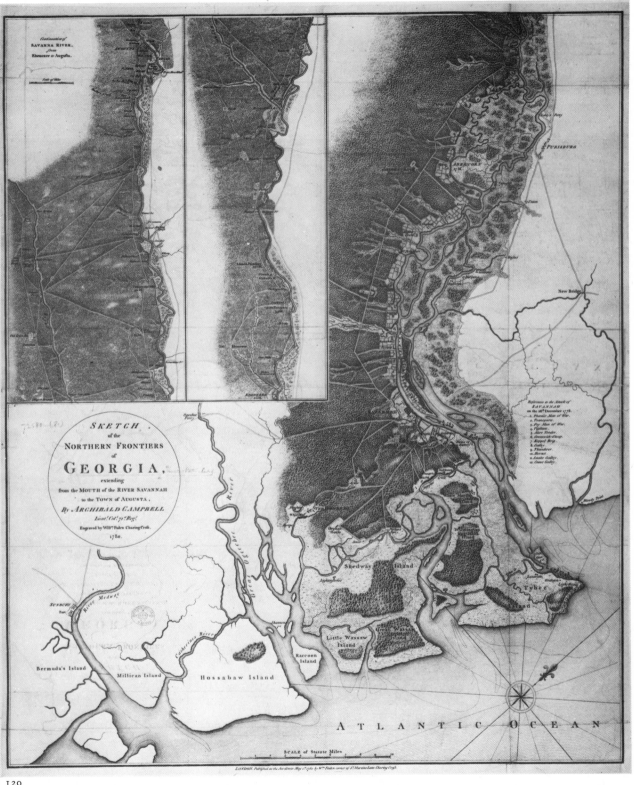

SKETCH
of the
NORTHERN FRONTIERS
of
GEORGIA,
extending
from the MOUTH of the RIVER SAVANNAH
to the TOWN of AUGUSTA,
By ARCHIBALD CAMPBELL
Lieut.! Col.! 71.st Reg.t
Engraved by W.m Faden Charing Cross.
1780.

### 129 Campbell's Attack on Savannah, December 1778

Sketch of the Northern Frontiers of Georgia, extending from the Mouth of the River Savannah to the Town of Augusta, By Archibald Campbell Lieut! Col! 71st Regt. London: Wm. Faden, May 1st 1780

1:111,500 approx. 73 × 62cm

*BL Map Library* 72580. (8)

Outlined by Germain to Clinton as early as March 1778, the campaign against the South was to be inaugurated by an attack on Savannah, the capital of Georgia which was the youngest and weakest of the thirteen colonies. Commanded by Lieut. Col. Archibald Campbell, the author of this map, 3,500 men escorted by Commodore Hyde Parker's squadron of warships arrived off Tybee Island at the mouth of the Savannah river on 23 December. On Boxing Day the troops were landed at Gerridoe's (Gerardo) Plantation, the first practicable landing place on the river. The American army, under Major-General Robert Howe, was drawn up to the east of Savannah, but guided by a Negro, some of Campbell's men were led through wooded swamps to the rear of Howe's forces. Attacked from front and rear, the Americans scattered in confusion; eighty three were killed, eleven wounded, and thirty more died in escaping through the swamps. British casualties numbered only three dead and ten wounded.

With the arrival of General Augustine Prevost and 2,000 more troops to reinforce Campbell's men, the town of Augusta was taken on 29 January 1779. Royal government and legislature was re-established in Georgia, and Sir James Wright arrived from England to resume the governorship, supported by local Loyalists.

### 130 His Majesty's Deluded Subjects

A Proclamation . . . whereas the Blessings of Peace, Freedom and Protection most graciously tendered by His Majesty to his deluded subjects of America; have been treated by Congress with repeated Marks of Studied Disrespect. . . Hyde Parker, Archibald Campbell.

36 × 21cm

*BL Department of Manuscripts Add. MS 34416.f.235*

Issued on 4 January 1779, only nine days after Savannah was taken, this Proclamation was signed by two officers who had quickly gained contrasting reputations. Over 400 prisoners had been taken since 26 December, and for lack of suitable quarters, they were placed on board ships, where many died of diseases during the following hot summer. Hyde Parker was hated by the Americans for his brutal manner and neglect of prisoners, while Campbell was respected for his generosity and humanity. Addressing the population as His Majesty's 'deluded subjects', the Proclamation invited all loyalists to join forces under the Royal Standard. Protection for families and possessions was promised in return for allegiance to the Crown, even deserters were offered full pardon if they surrendered within a specified time. Those who continued to oppose the re-establishment of 'legal' government, were warned of the miseries of the 'Rigours of War' for which they would be held responsible.

### 131 Oath of Allegiance to King George III, 1779

[A printed form of oath of allegiance to King George.] 'I [      ] do solemnly swear that I will bear true and faithful Allegiance to His Majesty King George the Third, my lawful Sovereign; . . . '

19 × 22cm

*BL Department of Manuscripts Add. MS 34416.f.236*

Following the Proclamation of 4 January 1779, several people came forward to swear allegiance to King George III. Proof of their support of the King was contained in a signed document by which they swore to 'solemnly disclaim and renounce that unlawful and iniquitous Confederacy, called the General Continental Congress'. Having given the oath 'without Equivocation, or mental Reservation', this certificate became a passport to protection and unrestricted travel to and from Savannah.

## 132 Savannah

A View of Savannah as it stood on the 29th March, 1734. To the Hon^ble the Trustees for establishing the Colony of Georgia in America This View of the Town of Savannah is humbly dedicated to their Honours Obliged and most obedient Servant, Peter Gordon.

39 × 54cm

*BL Map Library K. Top. CXXII.77.a*

Named in honour of King George II, and founded by General James Edward Oglethorpe in 1732 as a refuge for imprisoned debtors, Georgia was the youngest of the colonies. Situated at the edge of the colony, Savannah was still a frontier community in 1778, more than forty years after it was first established. 'Let the English reader picture to himself a town erected on the cliffs of Dover, and he will behold Savannah', wrote a contemporary British traveller. Taken in 1734, only a year after the town was founded in February 1733, this view of Savannah by Peter Gordon is the earliest known to exist.

## 133 The British Commander at the Siege of Savannah, 1779

Maj. Gen. Augustine Prevost. Colonel of the 60th. Foot. Died 1786.

Engraved portrait. 17 × 12cm

*BM Department of Prints and Drawings*
1936-12-7-192

General Augustine Prevost commanded the British army in Georgia and South Carolina during 1778 and 1779. Said to resemble George Washington in appearance, this 'diffident' but 'polite and disinterested' man was an experienced and courageous soldier, scarred from wounds received while serving under Wolfe at Quebec. Lieut.-Col. Campbell's opinion of him as a 'worthy man, but too old and inactive for this service', was substantiated by Prevost himself when he wrote from Savannah: 'I begin to feel the effect of age, and find that this campaign necessitates the greater physical powers of a younger man.' Replaced in 1780 by Clinton's arrival off Charleston, Prevost, who had been accorded 'distinguished applause' for the 'wisdom, vigilance and courage' which he displayed during the siege of Savannah, died in 1786.

## 134 The Siege of Savannah

Plan of the Town of Savannah, Shewing the Works Constructed for its Defence also, the Approaches and Batteries of the Enemy Together with the Joint Attack of the French & Rebels on the 9th October 1779. From a Survey by John Wilson 71st Regt. Asst. Engineer. [Signed by] James Moncrief Com^dt Engineer.

76 × 113cm

*BL Department of Manuscripts Add. MS 57716.3*

Early in September 1779 a French naval fleet, commanded by Charles-Henri, Compte d'Estaing, appeared off the coast of Georgia. It carried 4,000 French troops, prepared to join the Americans, under General Benjamin Lincoln, in destroying British power in the southern colonies, then centred at Savannah. D'Estaing demanded the surrender of the town. Prevost was granted twenty-four hours to consider the demand, during which time, Lieut.-Col. Maitland arrived from Port Royal with 800 men and Savannah's defences were strengthened. So strong were Prevost's lines that the allies, bringing up guns from the fleet, could make only gradual approaches to the British entrenchments. The bombardment of Savannah from land and river began on 4 October. The main and final assault of 9 October was repulsed with a loss to the allies of 800 dead and wounded, while British casualties numbered only about 150. Gathering storms then forced

D'Estaing to embark his fleet and Lincoln was forced to raise the siege and march off to Charleston.

The defeat of the allies was significant. The Royal Governor of Georgia wrote: 'I clearly saw that if this Province then fell, America was lost.' General Prevost's troops had 'preserved the Empire'. London celebrated the defeat of the allies by firing the Tower guns. New York would have been the only foothold left to George III in his American colonies had Georgia been lost, but this victory now allowed the transfer of the main theatre of war to the south.

John Wilson, author of this plan, a volunteer in the 71st Regiment, was ordered to do duty as an Assistant Engineer in May 1778.

For Colour Plate, see p. 95

### 135 Mouzon's map of North and South Carolina, 1775

An Accurate Map of North and South Carolina With Their Indian Frontiers, Shewing in a distinct manner all the Mountains, Rivers, Swamps, Marshes, Bays, Creeks, Harbours, Sandbanks and Soundings on the Coasts . . . the whole from Actual Surveys by Henry Mouzon and Others. London: Robt. Sayer and J. Bennett, May 30th 1775.

1:537,000 approx. 103 × 143cm

*BL Map Library* 1. *TAB.* 44. (35 and 36)

Used by American, French and British Forces, this large map by Henry Mouzon has been called the Revolutionary War map of North and South Carolina. George Washington's copy of the map was folded and clothbacked for saddle-bag use and copies were also possessed by Lieut.-Gen. J. B. D. de Vimeur Rochambeau and General Henry Clinton. Mouzon's map, published on the eve of the War, was closely based on Collet's *A Compleat Map of North Carolina from an actual survey* (1770) and became the main source for most maps of North Carolina until the early nineteenth century. His additional information included in particular more detailed accurate topography to the west

of the Catawba river. Mouzon derived his map of South Carolina from two earlier surveys: *A Map of South Carolina* . . . by Lodge-Cook (1771) and *A Map of the Province of South Carolina* . . . by James Cook (1773), both of which had a common source in *A Map of South Carolina and Part of Georgia* (1757) by the famous William Gerard de Brahm, Surveyor General to the Province of South Carolina.

### 136 The British Arrive at Charleston

A Plan of the Town, Bar, Harbour and Environs of Charlestown in South Carolina, with all the Channels, Soundings, Sailing-marks, etc. From the Surveys made in the Colony. London: Wm. Faden, June 1st 1780.

1:46,500 approx. 69 × 53cm

*BL Map Library RUSI A*30/31

Published on 1 June 1780, less than three weeks after the capitulation of the Americans at Charleston was signed, this map shows the location of the first great British Offensive since 1777. Sir Henry Clinton and 8,500 troops, accompanied by a fleet under Vice-Admiral Marriot Arbuthnot, sailed southward in December 1779. Landing near Johns Island about thirty miles from Charleston on 11 February 1780, the army took six weeks to advance from Johns to James Island, over Wappoo Cut, crossing Ashley river by the ferry until they finally arrived on Charleston neck on 29 March. This slow procession had given the provincials time to strengthen and enlarge the defences of Charleston. It was now well defended on the only side on which it could be approached by land.

On the seaward side the town was protected, firstly by a formidable sandbank, the Charleston bar at the mouth of the estuary of the Ashley, Wando and Cooper rivers; and secondly by the covering fire from Fort Moultrie on Sullivan's Island. In order to pass the bar the British ships unloaded their guns, provisions and water. The fleet passed Fort Moultrie with small loss. Whipple, the American Commodore, retreated

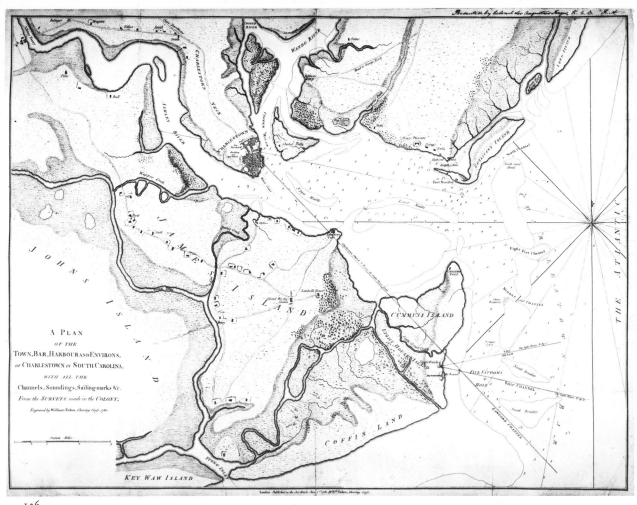

to Charleston with his ships, some of which he stationed in the Cooper river and the remainder he sunk across the mouth, thus preventing the British fleet from entering and bombarding the town from that side.

### 137 The Siege of Charleston, 1780

[Plan of Charleston.] MS unsigned, undated.

*c.*1:28,000. 55 × 76cm

*BL Department of Manuscripts Add. MS*
*57715.19*

Clinton's army soon finished the construction of their first trench or parallel and the town was now besieged by sea and land. The summons of the British commanders to the Americans to surrender was answered defiantly by General Lincoln: 'Sixty days have passed since it has been known that your intentions against this town were hostile, in which time has been afforded to abandon it, but duty and inclination point to the propriety of supporting it to the last extremity.' The British immediately bombarded the town, which still maintained communications with the open country to the east of the Cooper River. This route, by which Lincoln expected a reinforcement of 9,000 men, was later blocked and occupied by an army commanded by Earl Cornwallis.

The Charleston garrison, unable to retreat in any direction, now called a council of war and offered a conditional surrender of the town, the terms of which were rejected by Clinton. The besiegers pushed forward and the British again demanded an unconditional surrender in an attempt to save bloodshed, but were in turn rejected. The guns of the third and closest parallel trench then opened on the town, caus-

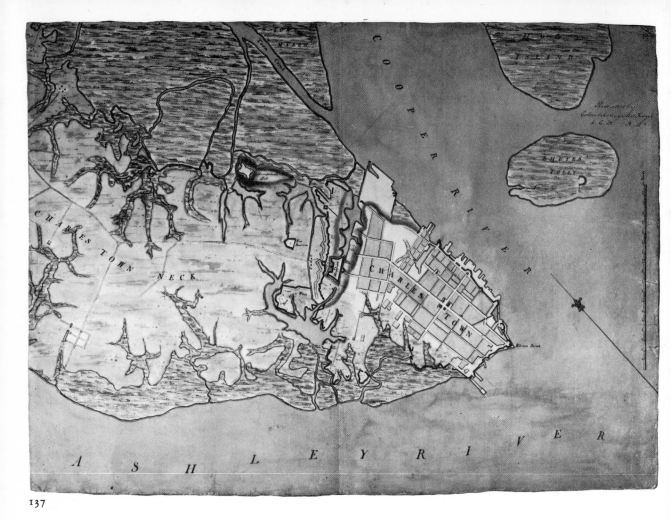

137

ing enormous destruction; Hessian riflemen commenced a devastating rifle fire, killing many of the Americans at their batteries. After two days of ceaseless firing the inhabitants petitioned General Lincoln to concede defeat. He wrote to Clinton on 11 May surrendering the town and his entire command; the capitulation being signed on 12 May. Shortly afterwards Lincoln was replaced by General Horatio Gates.

### 138 Conditions in Charleston under Siege, 1780

Copy of an intercepted Letter from B. Smith, to Mrs. Benjamin Smith, Dated Charles-Town, 30th April 1780. South Carolina: Robertson, MacDonald and Cameron, May 11 1780.

36 × 23cm

*BL Department of Manuscripts, Add. MS 34417.f.49*

Intercepted and published on Sir Henry Clinton's orders, this letter was written during the siege of Charleston by one of its inhabitants. Reassuring his wife, living outside the town, that he was still alive, Benjamin Smith wrote: 'Our Affairs are daily declining and not a Ray of Hope remains to assure us of Success.' The situation of the town rapidly became desperate once Cornwallis had cut off all communications to the east: 'This Letter will run great Risk, as it will be surrounded on all sides.' Food and fuel stocks were almost depleted. The Lieut.-Governor, Christopher Gadsden, and his council had pleaded with Lincoln not to abandon the town, but the longer he remained, the more dangerous became his position. It soon became apparent that there was nothing to prevent Lincoln's surrender but 'a Point of Honour in holding out to the last Extremity'.

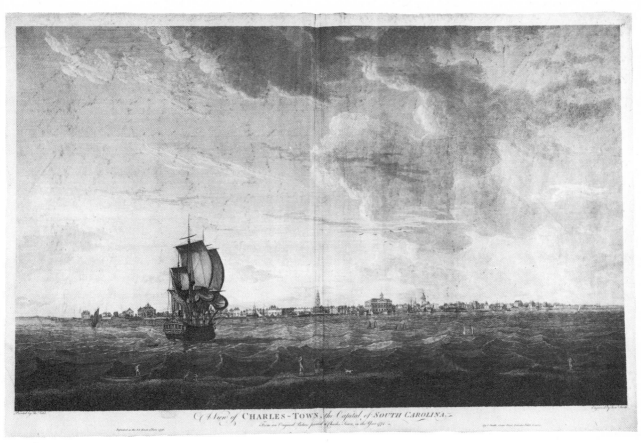

*A View of CHARLES-TOWN, the Capital of SOUTH CAROLINA.*

139

## 139 Charleston

A View of Charles-Town, the Capital of South Carolina. From an Original Picture painted of Charles Town, in the year 1774. Painted by Thos. Leitch. Engraved by Saml. Smith. London, 3rd June 1776.

48 × 74cm

*BL Map Library K. Top. CXXII.69*

Established in 1680 as the seat of government of the Carolinas, Charleston (originally spelled Charlestown), pictured here on the eve of the revolution, was South Carolina's only city throughout the colonial period. Located on the best Atlantic coast harbour south of Virginia, it was also the most important city in the whole of the south during the eighteenth century. As it monopolized the social, commercial and political life of the region, its fall in 1780 was a major catastrophe for America, following the loss of Savannah and the failure of the French and Americans to retake the city. Charleston's capture was for the British a great and inexpensive victory.

## 140 General Cornwallis (1738–1805)

Portrait of Charles, first Marquis and second Earl Cornwallis. By Thomas Gainsborough.

75 × 63cm

*Lent by the National Portrait Gallery*

Unlike most eighteenth-century British officers, Cornwallis had studied his profession. Travelling on the continent with a Prussian officer, he also studied at the Military Academy at Turin. A determined Whig, he was one of four peers who had opposed the resolution asserting the right of taxation in America. In spite of his political convictions, his deep sense of loyalty to the Crown was recognized by the King. Promoted to Major-General in 1775, he accepted a command to take reinforcements to Lord Howe in Halifax, Nova Scotia, in 1776. Participating in the operations on Long Island, the Battle of Brooklyn and the capture of New York, he went on to win victory at the Battle of Brandywine, 13 September 1776. The successful occupation of Philadelphia on 28 September saw the end of his first tour in America, and he returned home on leave to be promoted to Lieutenant-General. Sailing to America again in April 1778, he took up the post of second-in-command to Sir Henry Clinton, who had replaced Lord Howe as Commander-in-Chief in America. Disagreeing with Clinton on strategic policy, he submitted his resignation which the King refused to accept. News of his wife's illness then induced him to return to England, and on her death in February 1779 he again offered his services to the King and reached New York in August. He was in time to accompany Clinton on his expedition to Charleston, and assumed command of the army in the South on Clinton's return to New York in June 1780.

### 141 The Battle of Camden 16 August 1780

Sketch of the disposition and commencemt of the Action near Camden in South Carolina 16th August 1780. As discribed in the Letters of the Right Honble Earl Cornwallis to the Secretary of State: and the Rebel Gates to Congress. Most respectfully inscribed to the Right Honble. Earl Percy, by his Lordships most Humble Servant Ed. Barron.

MS 20 × 25cm

*Lent by His Grace the Duke of Northumberland*

The new Southern Army commanded by Gates, the victor of Saratoga, relied heavily on raw militia and lacked cavalry. Disregarding the advice of his colleague, Baron de Kalb, to advance westward, where supplies were relatively plentiful, Gates marched his starved troops straight to Camden, the main British

supply depot in the interior. Cornwallis, aware of the threat to his outpost, hurried from Charleston 150 miles away, confronting the American army at dawn on 16 August. Gates, abandoning his former military expertise, deployed his troops in an inexplicable manner. Instead of combining his untrained militia with Baron de Kalb's famous Continentals, he separated them, exposing the untrained irregulars along the entire left flank of the American line. As the British swept forward the American militia turned and 'ran like a torrent and bore all before them'. Eventually the Continentals were forced to give way, pursued by Cornwallis's cavalry. The extent of the rout is shown by the fact that on the same evening, Gates reported the battle from Charlotte, seventy miles from Camden.

The death of de Kalb, and the loss of yet another American army combined to make this the worst defeat ever suffered by the Patriots. Gates's conduct was questioned by Congress, and he was replaced by Nathanael Greene. Cornwallis's reports of the battle dated 20 and 21 August, from which Edward Barron drew his information for this plan of the battle, were published in the *London Gazette Extra* for 9 October 1780.

For Colour Plate, see p. 95

### 142 Horatio Gates (1728–1806)

Portrait of Horatio Gates. By C. W. Peale.

Photograph of the original in the Independence National Historical Park Collection.

Born in England, Gates adopted the patriot cause in 1775, and as a friend of Washington was commissioned Adjutant-General of the Continental Army with the rank of Brigadier-General. Following his victory at Saratoga, Gates decided to resign on the grounds of old age, but was elected President of the Board of War in 1777. After the failure of the Conway Cabal, a conspiracy to establish him in Washington's place, he tried in 1778 to make Washington displace Sullivan in his favour in the

Rhode Island expedition, but as Nathanael Greene noted, 'the General did not think proper to supersede an officer of distinguished merit by a doubtful friend'.

Directed by Congress to take command of the Southern Army in June 1780, against Washington's advice, he reached Rugeley's Mill, near Camden on 15 August. Here he was decisively beaten by Cornwallis. When Congress received news of the disaster in October, it demanded an inquiry, suspending Gates from office. Nathanael Greene, who relieved him on 2 December, treated Gates with the utmost kindness, refusing to hold a court of enquiry. Meanwhile the Virginia House of Delegates assured him that his previous glorious services could not be obliterated by any reverse of fortune. Only after 5 August 1782 was Gates's self-respect restored, when Congress revoked its demand for an enquiry. He spent the rest of the war with Washington at the cantonment at Newburgh.

## 143 The battle of Kings Mountain, 7 October 1780

The Journal of Alexander Chesney, a Loyalist, 1772–82.

MS 29cm

*BL Department of Manuscripts Add. MS 32627.f.16*

A staunch adherent to the Crown, Alexander Chesney became a lieutenant in the loyal militia after the fall of Charleston, when Clinton issued a proclamation summoning the King's supporters to enlist. Joining Major Patrick Ferguson's loyalist troops, he was promoted to captain in August 1780. Ferguson's force formed the left wing of Cornwallis's advance north through the Carolinas. His orders were 'to skirr [*sic*] the mountain country between the Catawba and the Yadkin, harass the Whigs, inspirit the Tories and embody the militia under the royal banner'. Ferguson aroused the wrath of the frontiersmen who poured through the mountain passes, uniting with other settlers from North

Carolina and Virginia. Realizing that he could not stand against them, Ferguson swiftly moved south, calling on Cornwallis for reinforcements. The backwoodsmen, led by Colonels Isaac Shelbey, William Campbell and John Savier, caught up with the loyalist forces at Gilberttown. Retreating to the summit of King's Mountain, Ferguson hoped to hold out until relief came from Cornwallis, but while preparing to defend his position, he was suddenly attacked on 7 October by riflemen 'who were well mounted and of course could move with the utmost celerity'. As Chesney remarked, 'so rapid was their attack that I was in the act of dismounting to report that all was quiet'. American ability with firearms and their knowledge of the terrain often made up for their lack of formal training, and King's Mountain was a classic example. 'Kings Mountain from its height would have enabled us to oppose a superior force with advantage', wrote Chesney, 'had it not been covered with wood which sheltered the Americans and enabled them to fight in their favourite manner.' Ferguson and more than 150 of the Loyalists were killed. Jefferson referred to the battle as 'the joyful annunciation of that turn in the tide of success that terminated the Revolutionary War with the seal of our Independence'. Cornwallis then decided to withdraw from North Carolina and winter south of Camden.

Alexander Chesney survived the battle and was one of the many Loyalists who journeyed to London after the war, seeking compensation for losses incurred while supporting the King. He eventually settled in Ireland.

## 144 The First British Military Breech-loading Rifle, c. 1776

Ferguson rifle.
Overall length 47½ inches
Barrel 43 inches
Calibre ·560
Rifling seven grooves

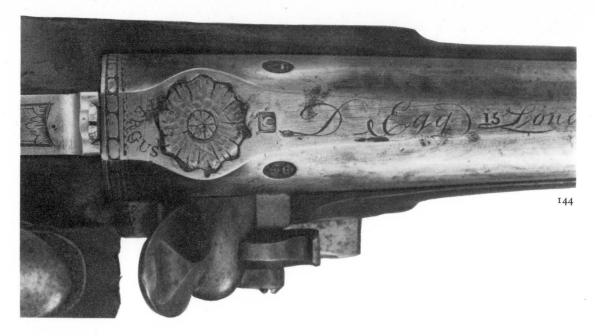

144

Maker, D. Egg, London

*Lent by Mr W. Keith Neal*

On the outbreak of war with the colonies in 1775, Captain Ferguson, then of the 70th Regiment, invented a new rifle to meet the challenge of the superior shooting of the American backwoodsmen. An accomplished marksman himself, Ferguson first demonstrated the rifle before Lord Townshend, Master General of the Ordnance, in 1776, and later before the King at Windsor. While claiming that its ingenious breech-loading mechanism would allow him to load and fire seven times a minute, he added 'that he could not undertake in that time to knock down above five of his Majesty's enemies'. The patent of 2 December 1776 covered several forms of breech action and 'various improvements upon firearms whereby they are loaded with more ease, safety and expedition, fire with more certainty and possess other advantages'.

This example of the rifle shows the word 'FERGUS' stamped behind the breech and above it a 'crescent or rising from a cloud proper'. This was the crest of Ferguson of Pitfour (the inventor). The company number 15 on the barrel indicates that it was intended to be used by his Corps. D. Egg was the principle contractor for the rifles designed and ordered by Ferguson. This rifle also shows the first form of backsight, exactly like the Patent Specification; this was soon altered and placed further down the barrel. The rifle is made to take a bayonet (missing), and has the side sling swivel at the butt end, which was another of Ferguson's improvements. The mounts are of very light coloured brass or tutaneg, better than average quality. It seems probable that this was one of the rifles which Ferguson owned or used in his famous trial before the Board of Ordnance.

### 145 Patrick Ferguson (1744–80)

Photograph, *c.*1880, of the bust of Colonel Ferguson, then in the possession of Mr Ferguson of Kinmundy.

44 × 39cm

*Lent by Mr W. Keith Neal*

'A born commander', Ferguson was apparently educated at the Royal Military Academy at Woolwich and obtained his first post at the early age of fourteen as a cornet in the Scots Greys. Acquiring his military experience on the battlefields of Germany and in the West Indies, he volunteered for service in America in 1776. He was given command of his own Rifle Corps, which was armed with his new invention, the breech-loading rifle. The battle of Brandywine demonstrated the effectiveness of the Corps, but Sir William Howe, annoyed at not having been consulted over its formation, used the serious wound Ferguson received in his right arm as an excuse to disband the force and return the rifles to store. After the fall of Charleston in 1780, Ferguson, now a major in the 71st Highlanders, was selected to marshall the loyalist militia over a large tract of country in which many of the Loyalists were themselves immigrants from Scotland. Displaying exceptional ability in both civil and military administration, Cornwallis appointed him brevet Lieut.-Col. He was again given an independent command of a force of loyalist volunteers, known as 'Ferguson's Sharpshooters'. His death a few months later at the battle of King's Mountain was keenly regretted by Cornwallis.

## 146 Daniel Morgan (1736–1802)

Portrait of Daniel Morgan, by C. W. Peale.

Photograph of the original in the Independence National Historical Park Collection.

Commissioned on 22 June 1775 as Captain of one of the two companies of riflemen to be raised in Virginia, Daniel Morgan accompanied Arnold's expedition to Quebec. He was also present at Bemis Heights with General Gates, having been promoted Colonel of a Virginia regiment. His refusal to participate in the intrigues against Washington later led to an estrangement between him and Gates.

Known as the 'old wagoner' after a former occupation, the redoubtable Virginia woodsman was distinguished as an able, bold, and successful leader of smaller patriot forces. Resigning in 1779 because of ill-health, he retired to Virginia, but General Greene, searching for capable subordinates with a 'knowledge of the Southern States and of the customs and manners of the inhabitants' recalled Morgan to active service in 1780.

Promoted to Brigadier-General, he was given the command of the forces in western North Carolina, which were opposing the advance of the British northward from Charleston. He won a brilliant victory at the battle of Cowpens (17 January 1781), for which he was awarded a gold

medal by Congress. Ill-health again led to his retirement shortly after joining Greene at Guildford Court House, but he later joined Lafayette briefly in the defence of Virginia in July 1781.

## 147 Nathanael Greene (1742–86)

Portrait of Nathanael Greene, by C. W. Peale.

Photograph of the original in the Independence National Historical Park Collection.

The fourth commander of the Southern Department in two years, Greene was a Rhode Islander who had never travelled further south than the Potomac river. A fervent nationalist, he condemned the 'prejudices of local attachments', declaring 'For my part I feel the cause and not the place. I would as soon go to Virginia as stay here' (in New England).

Faced with the task of reorganizing the Southern Army in the winter of 1780, he was careful to inform the guerrilla commanders Sumter, Morgan and Marion, that they would not be subordinated to Continental Army officers. Emphasizing the importance of coordinated action he stressed that 'you may strike a hundred strokes and reap little benefit from them, unless you have a good Army to take advantage of your success'.

Greene won remarkable achievements in his southern campaign with a poorly equipped army, rough partisan bands and undisciplined militia. He gave a classic example of American strategy, retreating as far as the British would pursue; and when the enemy, far from base, was forced to turn back, he would turn also and become the pursuer. 'There are few generals', he remarked 'who have run oftener ... than I have done. But I have taken care not to run too far, and commonly have run as fast forward as backward, to convince our Enemy that we were like a Crab, that could run either way.' Inflicting a severe defeat on the British at Eutaw Springs in September 1781, Greene ended the war by besieging Charleston, forcing the royal army to evacuate it on 14 December 1782.

Painted by Sir Joshua Reynolds    L^t COL. TARLETON.    Engraved by I. R. Smith

London, Publish'd Feb. 1 1782 by I. R. Smith, N^o 83, King's Bench, Covent Garden

148

### 148 Lieutenant-Colonel Banastre Tarleton (1754–1833)

Portrait of Banastre Tarleton, after Sir Joshua Reynolds.

Photograph of the original in the British Museum, Department of Prints and Drawings

Commissioned as a cornet in the King's Dragoon Guards in April 1775, Tarleton arrived in America as a volunteer in May 1776. His military prowess was soon recognized, and Sir Henry Clinton selected him for the post of Lieut.-Col. Commandant of the British Legion. Accompanying Clinton on the southern campaign, he achieved repeated successes against the Americans which won him praise from Clinton and Cornwallis. After the battle at Waxhaws (29 May 1780), where he almost annihilated a retreating column of Virginia Continentals, the Americans gave him the epithet 'Bloody Tarleton'.

In January 1781 Cornwallis prepared for a second advance into North Carolina and Tarleton's Legion was dispatched across the Enoree and Tiger rivers to harass Daniel Morgan's corps. Making a stand in the afternoon of 16 January at Cowpens, Morgan skilfully deployed his men, maximizing their sharpshooting abilities. Tarleton's force, worn out by an all night ride, arrived on the morning of the 17th. Tarleton foolishly ordered them to attack immediately, and the exhausted British were thoroughly beaten by Morgan's superior tactics. He had given the hated Tarleton 'a devil of a whipping, a more compleat victory was never obtained'. The British had lost more than half their men, the Americans only twelve dead and sixty wounded. The Cowpens debacle, following the defeat at King's Mountain, was another blow to British prestige in the south. Tarleton had lost his fearsome reputation, but continued to play a conspicuous part in the War until the surrender at Yorktown.

### 149 Simcoe's Journal

A Journal of the Operations of the Queen's Rangers, From the End of the Year 1777, to the Conclusion of the Late American War. By Lieutenant-Colonel Simcoe, Commander of that Corps. Exeter; Printed for the Author [1787].

28cm

*BL Department of Printed Books* 194.*a*.18

John Graves Simcoe (1752-1806) was promoted to Major-Commandant of the new provincial corps, the Queen's Rangers (Hussars) on 15 October 1777, and he was among the troops surrendering with Cornwallis at Gloucester Point in 1781. His journal was published about six years later with the aim of demonstrating the utility of a light corps or 'the service of a partizan'. A light corps was seen as a microcosm of the army as a whole, often operating in isolation, where the commanding officer would 'in his small sphere make use of the same principles which Generals apply to the regulations of armies'.

This copy of the journal was presented to George III by the author, whose accompanying MS letter, dated 15 March 1789, is bound into the volume together with manuscript maps and illustrations. Also included is a copy of a letter originally addressed to the Secretary at War, written 'during the period when the affairs of Holland seem'd to threaten this country with a continental War'. The letter contained a proposal to raise a corps at home, similar to that of the Queen's Rangers, which would operate in peace time as well as in war, thereby affording continuous military training in preparation for the defence of the country if threatened with invasion. Attempting to win the support of the King, Simcoe wrote: 'My ideas are that one of His Majesty's sons should be at the Head of this corps.' And the Prince 'would have studied the country and waged an imaginary war . . . with the best of Maps', so that it could be said: 'The son of our King is at the Head of the Army, and he will know how to give every hedgerow, and every rivulet its proper efficacy.'

The petition was unsuccessful, but Simcoe went on to become the first Lieutenant-Governor of Upper Canada in 1791.

For Colour Plate, see p. 94

JACK ENGLAND Fighting the FOUR CONFEDERATES.

150

## 150 The Opponents in 1781

Jack England Fighting the Four Confederates.
London: Printed for Jon. Smith, Robt. Sayer
& Jon. Bennett, Jany. 20, 1781.

17 × 23cm

*BM Department of Prints and Drawings, Satires*
5828

This cartoon, showing an English sailor facing
Holland, France, Spain and America, represents
the political situation at the beginning of 1781.
British victories against the allies in Georgia and
South Carolina together with naval supremacy
along the coast had left the Americans with
severe shortages of cash and equipment. Even
before the Franco-American alliance of 1778,
the French had supported the colonies. By 1781
French aid totalled $2,852,000. Spain, as the
ally of France, and hoping to profit from the
War by retaking Gibraltar from the British, had
also advanced considerable sums. Although
avowedly neutral, the Dutch had been shipping
arms to America and thus the declaration of war
on Holland in December 1780 was regarded with
relief by the British navy since Holland was 'less
troublesome as a declared enemy than as a very
nominal neutral'.

## 151 The Battle at Guildford Court House, 15 March 1781

Battle of Guildford, Fought on the 15th of
March 1781.

In: C. Stedman, *History of the American War*.
London, 1794.

1:18,000 approx. 28cm

*BL Department of Printed Books* 601.1.21

The great improvement in American fortunes
which occurred after the resounding defeat of
Tarleton at Cowpens determined Cornwallis to
salvage British prestige in the South by any
expedient, 'however desperate'. Pursuing Morgan across country he reached Ramsours Mill
on 25 January, but finding his prey still beyond
his grasp he made the highly unorthodox decision to abandon his heavy equipment, food and
baggage, in an effort to transform his troops
into a swiftly mobile unit. General Greene, who
had sped to join forces with Morgan, then led
Cornwallis on a memorable chase through
North Carolina. Greene finally took up position
on 14 March at Guildford Court House, in preparation for a formal battle. Cornwallis, who
was now several hundred miles from base,
promptly attacked Greene on the morning of
15 March. The American general adopted similar tactics to those used by Morgan at Cowpens,
and both armies fought hard at the three successive lines of battle shown on the map. The outcome of the fight became uncertain, and Greene
decided to retreat rather than gamble on a decisive victory, especially as the alternative of
defeat would be heavy and costly.

Thus Cornwallis gained a victory, but at
great expense, losing about 500 dead and wounded, and his weakened army did not have the
strength to pursue the Americans and consoli-
date the victory.

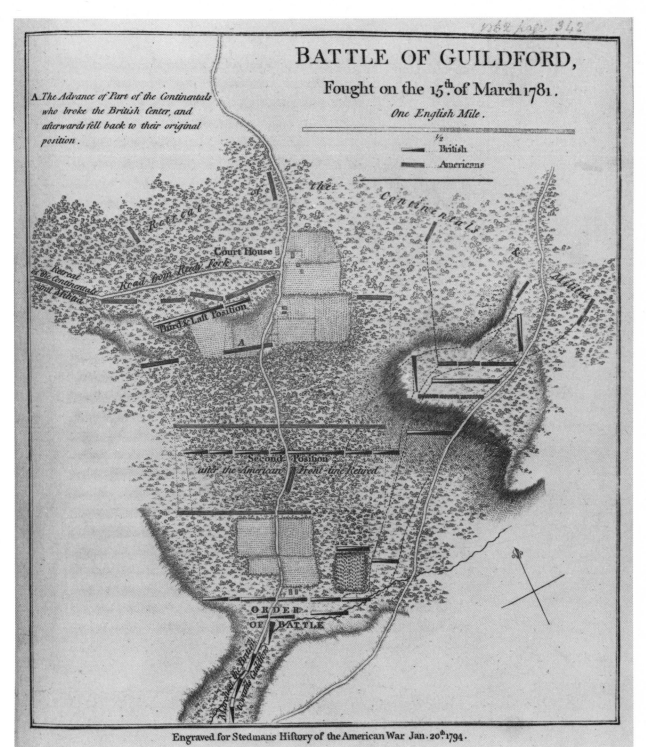

A. The Advance of Part of the Continentals who broke the British Center, and afterwards fell back to their original position.

BATTLE OF GUILDFORD,

Fought on the 15th of March 1781.

One English Mile.

½

British

Americans

Court House

Road from Reedy Fork

Third & Last Position

A

Retreat of the Continentals

Retreat of the Continentals and Militia

Second Position after the American Front-line Retired

ORDER OF BATTLE

Continentals & Militia

March of the British towards Guildford

Engraved for Stedmans History of the American War Jan. 20th 1794.

151

After the battle at Guildford Court House, Cornwallis planned to march into Virginia, leaving Greene free to attack the British troops remaining in South Carolina and Georgia. About 8,000 strong, they were commanded by Lord Rawdon, who at twenty-six was the same age as Tarleton, but was a veteran of the War since Bunker Hill.

Intent on diverting his opponent while the partisans struck at the seven forts ringing Charleston, Greene drew up his forces on Hobkirk's Hill, about two miles north of Camden. Lord Rawdon advanced with 1,500 men and attacked the Americans on 25 April. The Americans, numerically superior and placed in a strong defensive position, initially gained the upper hand, but it was typical of most of Greene's engagements in the South that he was finally beaten and forced to retreat. He remarked afterwards to the French Minister, La Luzerne, 'We fight, get beat, rise, and fight again', and it was soon apparent that the sum of his lost battles was victory in an effective war of attrition.

### 153 The Holster Atlas

The American Military Pocket Atlas; being An approved Collection of Correct Maps, Both General and Particular, of the British Colonies; Especially those which now are, or probably may be The Theatre of War. . . London: R. Sayer and J. Bennet, [1776].

23cm

*BL Department of Printed Books* G19, 826

'Taken principally from the actual surveys and judicious observations of engineers De Brahm and Romans . . . and other officers, employed in His Majesty's Fleet and Armies', this portable atlas, containing six folding maps, was issued to British officers for use in the field during the War of Independence. The royal forces benefitted from a considerable collection of official maps prepared both before and during the War by trained military engineers. In contrast, the Americans, as Washington noted, initially suf-

pcint par Wickenson a Boston
### GENERAL ARNOLD
*Qui avec le General Gates avoit de environer le General Lieu-tenant Bourgoyne, que toute l'Armée se rendît Prisoniere, et l'obligea de mettre bas les Armes.*
*Se vend a Londres chez Thom: Hart.*

154

### 152 Lord Rawdon Defeats General Greene

Sketch of the Battle of Hobkirk's Hill, near Camden, on the 25th April, 1781.

*In*: C. Stedman, *History of the American War*, London, 1797.

No scale 44 × 30cm

*BL Department of Printed Books*
601. l. 21

fered from the 'want of accurate Maps of the Country. . . . I have in vain endeavoured to procure them, and have been obliged to make shift, with such Sketches, as I could trace from my own Observations and that of Gentlemen around me.'

## 154 The Traitor and the Spy

A portrait of General Arnold peint par Wilkenson à Boston. Se vend a Londres chez Thom Hart [1780?]

38 × 31cm

*BM Department of Prints and Drawings,* 1902-10-11-7068

155 A portrait of Major John André, late Adjutant General to the British Army in North America. Dodd delin. Cook sculp.

Engraved for Raymond's *History of England,* 1794

38 × 31cm

*BM Department of Prints and Drawings,* 1872-11-19-155

On 3 August 1780, after weeks of anxious and repeated requests, Washington allowed Major-General Benedict Arnold (1741–1801) to take command of the garrison at West Point, on the Hudson River, the key to communication between New England and the northern colonies. Unwittingly, Arnold was also given his long-awaited chance to betray the fort to the British. Arnold's betrayal stemmed from his treatment by Congress and the Army and from his wife's own fierce loyalism. The hero of Canada, Arnold was accused of extortion and peculation and his promotion to major-general was blocked until Saratoga, 1777, when, ironically, he was seriously wounded and disabled from active service. His unfortunate British accomplice was Sir Henry Clinton's *aide-de-camp* Major John André (1751–80). On the night of 21 September, André met Arnold to receive particulars about the defences of West Point

MAJOR JOHN ANDRE, Late Adjutant General to the British Army in North America.

155

and to arrange for a British attack. Making his way back to the British lines disguised as a civilian, André fell into American hands and incriminating evidence was found in his boot. He was hanged as a spy on 20 October 1780. Arnold fled to the British and took part in a number of ineffectual skirmishes before leaving in 1782 for England, where £6,000 compensation awaited him.

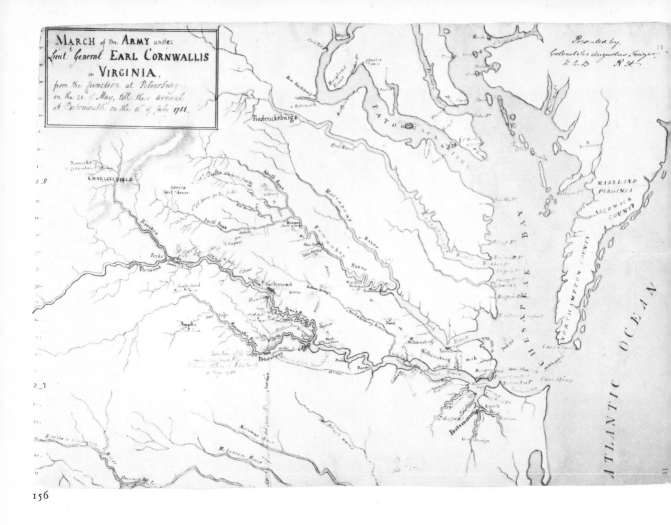

MARCH of the Army under Lieut. General EARL CORNWALLIS in VIRGINIA. from the junction at Petersburg on the 20 of May, till their arrival at Portsmouth on the 12th of July 1781.

156

### 156 The Marches of Lord Cornwallis in Virginia

March of the Army under Lieut. General Earl Cornwallis in Virginia, from the junction at Petersburg on the 20th of May, till their arrival at Portsmouth on the 12th of July 1781.

MS unsigned and undated.

No scale 39 × 55 cm

*BL Department of Manuscripts*
*Add. MS* 57715.11

Convinced 'that if offensive war is intended, Virginia appears . . . the only province in which it can be carried on', Cornwallis marched north from Wilmington on 25 April and arrived at Petersburg on 20 May. Here he joined forces with British raiding parties who, sent by Clinton, had been operating in Virginia since December 1780 under the command of Major-General William Phillips and the American

traitor, Benedict Arnold. Cornwallis then assumed command of the 5,000 strong British troops in Virginia at which Clinton, who had not given his subordinate firm orders to this effect, declared: 'My wonder at this move of Lord Cornwallis will never cease. But he has made it, and we shall say no more but make the best of it.' The Commander-in-Chief intended the war in Virginia to be defensive, except for 'desultry expeditions'.

This map, by an unknown cartographer, shows the routes followed by Cornwallis during his two months of indecisive campaigning in Virginia. Advancing beyond Richmond he destroyed American supply depots and tobacco warehouses. A raid on Charlottesville by Tarleton, sent Acting-Governor Jefferson and the Virginia legislature into ignominious flight after which Cornwallis returned towards Portsmouth.

# The Commonwealth of Virginia

To *Charles Creacroft Gentleman*                                                    Greeting:

**K**NOW you, that from the special Trust and Confidence which is reposed in your Patriotism, Fidelity, Courage, and good Conduct, you are, by these Presents, constituted and appointed *Major* of Militia in the County of *Monongalia* You are therefore carefully and diligently to discharge the Duty of *a Major* of the Militia, by doing and performing all Manner of Things thereunto belonging; and you are to pay a ready Obedience to all Orders and Instructions which from Time to Time you may receive from the Governor, or executive Power of this State for the Time being, or any of your superiour Officers, agreeable to the Rules and Regulations of the Convention or General Assembly. All Officers and Soldiers under your Command are hereby strictly charged and required to be obedient to your Orders, and to aid you in the Execution of this Commission, according to the Intent and Purport thereof.

Witness *Patrick Henry*, Esquire, Governour or Chief Magistrate of the Commonwealth, at *Williamsburg*, under the Seal of the Commonwealth, this *15th* Day of *March* in the *Third* Year of the Commonwealth, Annoq. Dom. 1779.

157

## 157 An Officer's Commission for the Virginia Militia

Appointment, by the Commonwealth of Virginia, of Charles Creacroft to the rank of Major in the Virginia militia. Signed by Patrick Henry, 15 March 1779.

23 × 40cm
*BL Department of Manuscripts
Add. MS 21842.f.170*

Signed by Patrick Henry, the Chief Magistrate of the Commonwealth of Virginia, this commission appointed 'Charles Creacroft, Gentleman' to the position of Major in the militia of the County of Monongalia. Predominant Whig thinking in Virginia at this time held that the militia constituted the 'cheapest and surest defence, on whose protection we are ultimately to depend'. Virginia was the only state in the South to have escaped the ravages of war, but the arrival of Cornwallis in 1781, and the strength of his amalgamated forces, now threatened the state with large-scale invasion. The militia were mobilized in an attempt to swell Lafayette's army when he arrived in Virginia. General Thomas Nelson of the militia became Thomas Jefferson's successor as Governor of the state, thereby combining military and civil authority, ensuring that the executive could work with 'more energy, promptitude and effect for the state'.

## 158 George Washington 1732–99

Oval medallion: Jasper ware on a blue ground and set in a brass frame. The head is in profile facing right. Impressed mark on the back: WEDGWOOD & BENTLEY

The model was taken from a medal designed by Voltaire and struck in Paris in 1777, and the plaque was in production in 1779.

Height: 3·6in, 91mm

Gift of Mr and Mrs Isaac Falcke, 1909

*BM Department of Medieval and Later Antiquities*, 1909, 12-1, 147

### 159 Marie Joseph, Marquis de Lafayette (1757–1834)

Portrait of Lafayette by C. W. Peale.

Photograph of the original in the Independence National Historical Park Collection.

Lafayette, a young French nobleman, espoused the American cause after learning of the Declaration of Independence, and arrived in Georgetown, South Carolina on 13 June 1777. To his offer of military services as a volunteer and at his own expense, Congress responded on 31 July by granting him the rank of major-general. Lafayette and Washington became firm friends and the French general was given the command of the division of Virginia light troops. Sharing the hardships and privations of the American forces during the bitter winter at Valley Forge, he earned the title of 'soldier's friend'.

After the French Alliance of 1 May 1778 Lafayette became invaluable as a liaison officer, and on his return to Paris on leave in January 1779 he was successful in urging the formation of a French expeditionary army to serve in America, to be commanded by Rochambeau. Having returned to Boston in March 1781 Lafayette was ordered south and arrived in Richmond, Virginia, in time to prevent its occupation and destruction by the British army under General Phillips. The inferior American troops had little success in harassing Lord Cornwallis's army in Virginia. Informing Lafayette of the proposed coordination of the allied forces against Cornwallis, Washington ordered the young general to hold Lord Charles in Virginia and prevent his escape. Describing the British capitulation at Yorktown on 19 October, Lafayette wrote to the Comte de Maurepas: 'The play is over, the fifth act is just ended.' Much fêted and by now famous, he returned to France in December 1781.

### 160 Jean Baptiste de Vimeur, Comte de Rochambeau (1725–1807)

Portrait of General Rochambeau, by C. W. Peale.

Photograph of the original in the Independence National Historical Park Collection

Appointed commander of the French expeditionary army to America, Rochambeau, a Brigadier-General and Inspector of Cavalry, displayed considerable administrative ability. He sailed with the French forces on 1 May 1780, arriving off Rhode Island on 11 July. Informing Washington of his arrival, Rochambeau wrote that the King's orders placed him at the disposal of the American Commander-in-Chief. The two Generals then learned that the Comte de Grasse had sailed with the French fleet to the West Indies, and would later join them. Rochambeau urged that instead of adopting Washington's plan to attack New York, the allies should mount an offensive against Cornwallis in Virginia.

On 14 August news arrived that de Grasse was sailing for the Chesapeake, and five days later Rochambeau and Washington began the long march south. General William Heath and 3,000 men were left in front of New York to deceive the enemy into thinking that the city was still the allies' main objective. The Franco-American armies travelled with great speed, and coordinated their movements and those of the two fleets with extraordinary skill. They arrived at Yorktown before Clinton had time to send reinforcements to Cornwallis, thus sealing the fate of the British in America.

### 161 The Siege of Yorktown, October 1781

[Plan of Yorktown and Gloucester, showing the British and Allied fortifications.] Signed John Hayman Lieut. 17th Infy. Dated Juliana 12th June 1782.

MS copy. No scale 66 × 54cm

*BL Department of Manuscripts*
*Add. MS* 15535.6

'The whole Army will march by the right in one column at 5 o'clock tomorrow morning precisely . . .' read Washington's General Orders,

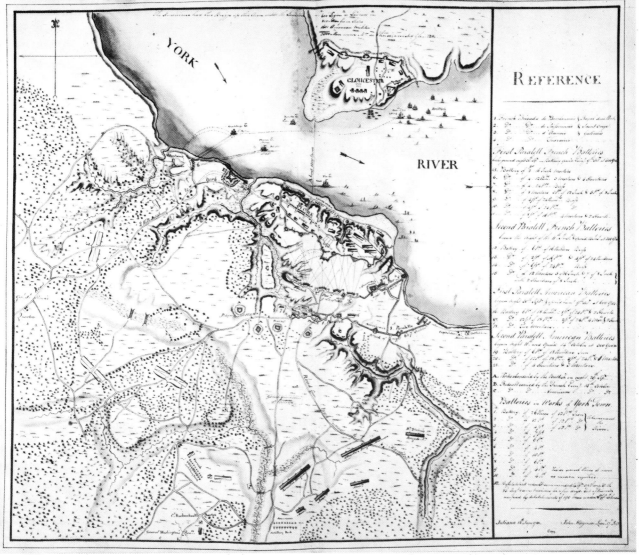

The REFERENCE panel on the right side of the map contains detailed annotations listing French and American batteries and works.

issued at Williamsburgh for the combined allied forces for 28 September 1781. The investment of Yorktown by the Americans and French had begun. Cornwallis hurriedly wrote to Clinton: 'This place is in no state of defence. If you cannot relieve me very soon, you must be prepared to hear the worst.' The British had been fortifying Yorktown since August 'a work of great time and labour', and the small town was ringed with trenches and redoubts. The settlement of Gloucester on the opposite bank of the York River had also been strengthened and was occupied by General O'Hara and Lieut.-Col. Tarleton's troops.

By 8 October the allied trenches and gun positions, shown on this map, were ready. Cornwallis had abandoned the outer defence works and retreated into the town. Lafayette's division took over the trenches on 9 October and heavy, accurate, artillery fire was opened on the beleaguered royal troops. On 15 October Cornwallis, who had been promised reinforcements by Clinton, wrote to his superior: 'The safety of this place is so precarious that I cannot recommend that the fleet and army should run great risk in endeavouring to save us.' He held out until 17 October when he sued for an amnesty.

162

## 162 'The World Turned Upside Down'

Reddition de L'Armée du Lord Cornwallis.
In: 'Recueil D'Estampes Représentant Les
Différens Evènemens de la Guerre qui a
procuré l'Indépendance aux Etats unis de
L'Amérique. A Paris chez M. Ponce. . . et
chez M. Godefroy. [1783].

24cm

*BL Department of Printed Books C.33.l.4*

The day following Cornwallis's request for
amnesty was spent in discussing the terms of
surrender, and before eleven o'clock on the
morning of 19 October the capitulation was
signed. The military honours which had been
denied the Americans at the fall of Charleston
were now denied the British. They marched out
of Yorktown with colours cased, and, according
to tradition, to the ironically appropriate
English air of, 'The World Turned Upside
Down'.

Count de Rochambeau, who was present at
the surrender, wrote: 'The garrison marched
out at two o'clock between the two armies,
drums beating, carrying their arms which were
stacked, with about twenty flags. Lord Cornwallis being ill, General O'Hara marched out at
the head of the garrison, when he approached
me he presented his sword. I pointed to General
Washington opposite me as the head of the
American army, and said to him that as the
French army was an auxilliary on this Continent, that it was now from the American General that he must take his orders.'

On hearing of the defeat of His Majesty's
forces at Yorktown, Lord North is reputed to
have groaned, 'Oh God! It is all over.'

163

## 163 Commemorative Medal, 1781

Libertas americana, 1781. Engraved in France
by Augustin Dupré, engraver at the French
Mint.

47mm diam

*BM Department of Coins and Medals*
*Betts* 615

The obverse shows a head of Liberty with flow-
ing hair; a staff and a liberty-cap behind the
head. The reverse shows the infant Hercules in
his shield-shaped cradle, who has strangled two
serpents which symbolize the battles of Saratoga and Yorktown. Hercules is still exposed to
the rage of the British Lion; but the lion, his
tail between his legs, is repelled by the lance of
Minerva, who holds a shield emblazoned with
the lilies of France.

### 164 Letter from Cornwallis

[Letter from Cornwallis to Balfour, dated New York 25 November 1781.] MS signed.

23 × 19cm

*Lent by Mr Thomas Tesoriero, New York*

Written only a week after Cornwallis had arrived in New York on parole in November 1781, this letter from him was addressed to Lieut.-Colonel Nisbet Balfour, then commandant at Charleston. Commenting that several of his letters had gone astray, Cornwallis referring to the disastrous capitulation at Yorktown only five weeks previously, wrote 'altho' I have been unfortunate I trust I have not been criminal'. Cornwallis knew that he enjoyed the public support of Germain, and shortly after his return to England in early January 1782, King George wrote to reassure him: 'the whole tenor of your conduct has so manifestly shown, that Attachment to My Person, to your Country, and to the Military Profession are the motives of Your Actions, that I am certain no fresh proof is necessary to the World for justice to be done you on that head'. Cornwallis continued on parole until 20 January 1783 when all prisoners were released on both sides after the signing of the preliminaries of peace.

# VI *The Making of Peace*

When King George III received Lord George Germain's news of the defeat at Yorktown, his note of acknowledgement betrayed only one sign of disturbance, as Germain observed: 'He has omitted to mark the hour and minute of his writing with his usual precision.' The King still hoped that with concerted measures for continuing the contest 'a good end may yet be made to this War'. The House of Commons determined otherwise. On 4 March 1782 they passed without a division a motion 'to consider as enemies to His Majesty and the Country all those who should advise or . . . attempt to further prosecution of offensive war on the continent of America'. Lord North was given leave to conclude a peace. 'At last the fatal day is come', the King wrote on 27 March 1782, on the news of North's resignation. With these debates and the ensuing ministerial changes began the long process of making a peace.

On the American side, Congress on 25 September 1779 had named John Adams as peace commissioner, and on 13-14 June 1781 appointed John Jay, Henry Laurens, Benjamin Franklin and Thomas Jefferson to join Adams in a five-man peace commission. As Jefferson declined to serve, Laurens was a prisoner in the Tower of London after his capture on the high seas, and Jay and Adams were delayed in their arrival in Paris, the initial discussions were in the hands of Franklin. Popularly known as 'the sage of Passy', throughout the negotiations Franklin dominated the scene, as New World philosopher, and a humanitarian of international reputation. Shelburne, Secretary of State with responsibility for America, sent to Paris as the British emissary his personal friend the Scotsman Richard Oswald, one time slave-owner, who had already been used by the government as a consultant on account of his American estates and business interests. In 1781 Oswald had stood £50,000 bail for Henry Laurens to secure his release, and had accompanied Laurens (under parole) to Haarlem to meet Adams as a commissioner for peace, going on to Paris to consult with Franklin. A Cabinet Minute of 25 April 1782 recommended that Oswald should return to Paris and open discussions for negotiating a general peace. Shelburne's rival, Charles James Fox, Secretary of State with responsibility for Europe, sent as his emissary to Paris Thomas Grenville, son of George Grenville of Stamp Act fame. Franklin's open preference for Oswald, disagreements between Oswald and Grenville, and finally Fox's resignation, led to Oswald's appointment as sole British negotiator. On the fall of Shelburne's ministry in February 1783 Oswald was replaced by Fox's nominee David Hartley. Throughout his thirteen months of negotiations Oswald was assisted by Caleb Whitefoord, an old friend of Franklin and his next-door neighbour in Craven Street during Franklin's five years residence in London. Characterized by Edmund Burke respectively as 'simple merchant' and 'a mere *diseur de bons mots*' Oswald and Whitefoord were more accomplished diplomats than Shelburne's enemies supposed. Of the cordial personal friendship between the members of the two commissions Adams remarked: 'We lived together in perfect good humour. Had we been merely on our travels, or on a party of pleasure, nothing could have been more agreeable.'

Despite her defeat on the American continent, Great Britain had certain advantages which she exploited to the full during the negotiations. The War had widened its horizons. Rodney's victories in the West Indies, Howe's relief of Gibraltar, and the campaigns in India brought new and complex considerations to the council tables. Rivalries and suspicions between the Allies were encouraged to advance British interests. Once the Cabinet had agreed on 19 September 1782 to the unquestioned acknowledgement of the United States 'as an independent power' and that Oswald be empowered to treat with 'the commissioners appointed by the Colonys, under the title of Thirteen United States', the way was clear for the negotiation of a preliminary treaty. The Articles of Peace between Great Britain and the United States were signed on 30 November 1782. On 20 January 1783, Great Britain signed preliminary treaties with the allies, France and Spain. The Definitive Treaty signed on 3 September 1783 ended the long months of negotiations.

The terms were moderate, and for the loyalists the best which could be obtained. For the territorial demarcations in America first class evidence of the intentions of the negotiators is provided by the 'Red-lined map' which was presented to King George III. This map comprised a copy of Mitchell's map of North America, 1775, marked by Oswald with the frontiers agreed for the Preliminary Articles of Peace. As the map was not included in the term of the treaty and inaccuracies were discovered on the printed map, further arbitration was required to determine disputed areas. When the Ashburton Treaty was negotiated in 1842 Great Britain kept the Red-lined map safely out of sight regarding it as too favourable to the American case. It was thought to reflect the American sympathies of Oswald as British negotiator.

'Blessed are the Peacemakers' was the theme of satirical comment from the cartoonists. The negotiators expected little thanks for their efforts, 'for of all menkind (wrote Whitefoord) none are so apt to be traduced vilified and misrepresented as your Peacemakers'. General Haldimand as Governor of Canada saw to the resettlement of the Loyalists in Canada, whose arrival set that country on a new course of destiny. There was consolation too in the fact that the new republic sprang from English stock. As Whitefoord pointed out to a French diplomat: 'He talk'd of the growing Greatness of America, and that the thirteen United States wou'd form the Greatest Empire in the world. "Yes Sir, I replied, and they will *all* speak English."' The report on the new republic sent to John Wilkes by Thomas Mullett in 1784 struck a similar note of hope that Great Britain and America might go forward in friendship and cooperation to their mutual advantage.

To King George III and to many of the active participants in the War on both sides of the Atlantic the outcome seemed a revolutionary overthrow of the old order of things. 'Tout, en ce monde, a été Révolution,' the Spanish Minister remarked to John Adams in 1783. A fitting final comment is the title of the song traditionally associated with Yorktown; 'The World Turned Upside Down'.

*Blessed are the PEACE MAKERS*

165

**165 Blessed Are the Peace Makers, 1783**

Engraving. Published by E. Dachery Feb^y
24 1783 St. James's Street.

22 × 33cm

*BM Department of Prints and Drawings,
Satires* 6174

Dachery's political satire on the Preliminaries of
Peace (signed on 20 January 1783) was published just after the violent attack on the peace
terms in the Commons on 17 February, followed by the fall of the Shelburne Ministry. It
shows the belligerent powers in procession
along a country road, Spain in the lead, followed by France, who holds the end of a rope tied
round the neck of George III. Behind the King
walks Shelburne, carrying the Preliminary
Articles of Peace. Behind them is America, who
holds aloft a scourge labelled *America*, with
which he is about to strike Shelburne and the
King. Last comes Holland, also led by the neck,
and depicted as a sulky boor.

169(a)

Peace shall be agreed upon between Gr: Britain & France . . . they are the best that the Circumstances of the Times woud admit of.' Caleb Whitefoord, in this letter to a London friend, goes on to complain: 'It is written, Blessed are the Peacemakers! & so it might have been in ancient Times but in those of modern Date on a changé tout cela & changed too with a Vengeance, for of all menkind none are so apt to be traduced vilified & misrepresented as your Peacemakers.'

Whitefoord, London merchant and dilettante, found himself in this unaccustomed role of diplomatist through his long friendship with Benjamin Franklin. Asked by the British Commissioner Richard Oswald to accompany him to Paris in April 1782 and to introduce Oswald to Franklin, he stayed in Paris for thirteen months until the end of April 1783, attending Oswald in the negotations and acting as sole secretary to the British Peace Commission.

### 166 The Peacemakers 1782

Letter from Caleb Whitefoord to Frederic Stuart dated 25 December 1782.

23 × 22cm

*BL Department of Manuscripts*
*Add. MS 36593 ff. 177–8*

'Tis some satisfaction, that our mission has not been in vain. The great Object of it was accomplish'd on St Andrews day, when we signd & seald the articles of a Preliminary Treaty with America, to take Effect whenever Terms of

### 167 Caleb Whitefoord's French Passport, 1783

A passport signed by King Louis XVI and the Comte de Vergennes for Caleb Whitefoord to travel through France on his return from Paris to London. Dated Versailles 24 April 1783.

34 × 22cm

*BL Department of Manuscripts*
*Add. MS 36593, f. 197*

On the fall of Lord Shelburne's ministry in February 1783 Charles James Fox, the new Foreign Secretary, took charge of the peace negotations and lost no time in replacing Shelburne's plenipotentiaries in Paris with his own nominees. Recalled to London for a few days in March, Oswald found himself replaced as Commissioner by David Hartley, and saw no reason to return to Paris. Armed with a passport from King Louis XVI valid for three weeks and carrying with him Oswald's papers as instructed by letter, Whitefoord returned to England at the end of April 1783.

**168 Letter from W. T. Franklin to Caleb Whitefoord, 7 August 1783**

*BL Department of Manuscripts*
*Add. MS 36593, ff. 202–3*

23 × 18cm

William Temple Franklin, Benjamin Franklin's grandson, served in Paris as secretary to his grandfather, and from 1 October 1782, acted as Secretary to the American Peace Commission. Writing to Caleb Whitefoord he regrets the changes following the fall of Shelburne's ministry. Fox, despite his professed liberalism, was proving an intractable negotiator in the matter of trade reciprocity. 'Our Negotiations do not go on so well as when Mr O. & you were here. We have lost by the Change a worthy Friend, & your Country, an able & upright Minister.'

**169 The Preliminary Articles of Peace between Great Britain and America, 30 November 1782**

*Lent by the Public Record Office F.O. 93/8/1*

'We met first at Mr Jay's, then at Mr Oswald's, examined & compared the Treaties . . . Then the Treaties were signed, sealed & delivered, & we all went out to Passy to dine with Dr. Franklin', John Adams wrote in his Journal for 30 November 1782.

Final talks to determine the Preliminary Articles of Peace between Great Britain and America had opened at Paris on 26 October 1782 between Adams, Franklin and Jay as American Commissioners and Richard Oswald representing Great Britain, assisted by Sir Henry Strachey, Shelburne's special envoy. The terms ratified on 30 November recognized in their first Article the independence of the United States of America (as demanded by the Americans) and in the second agreed boundaries which gave America 'little to complain of and not much to desire'. According to protocol Oswald signed first as representative of the most venerable state, the Americans then signing in alphabetical order, Adams, Franklin, Jay

169(b)

and Laurens. On the following page Whitefoord and W. T. Franklin signed as witnesses. Seals were affixed and signed originals handed to each side. Of these only the British one survives. Evidence suggest that although certified copies were taken to the United States, the original was never received there, but remained in the hands of the Commissioners in Paris and then disappeared. The separate Article concerning West Florida set out in the last page of the original document was supposed to be secret, but news of it soon became known.

**170 Signing the Preliminary Articles of Peace, 30 November 1782**

An unfinished oil painting by Benjamin West, 1784 (photograph courtesy of The Henry Francis du Pont Winterthur Museum).

'Some time ago, our old friend Mr. West having the opportunity of seeing three of the American Plenipo's here, & wishing to transmit their Portraits to Posterity in some Historical Picture, made a sketch of the signing of the Preliminary Treaty, to which I contributed part by lending him the Portrait of your Grandfather by Mr. Wright, which I brought with me from Paris', Caleb Whitefoord wrote to William Temple Franklin on 30 June 1784, requesting him to supply a portrait of himself as secretary of the American Commission. The portrait depicts the American signatories (left to right) Jay, Franklin (portrayed from various sources, not from life), and Adams, with Henry Laurens and W. T. Franklin in attendance. The blank space on the right hand was reserved for the British party, Oswald, Whitefoord, Strachey and Fitzherbert. There is a tradition that Richard Oswald, who was blind in one eye and felt a repugnance to having his portrait painted, declined to appear.

**171 A Confidential Report from Paris**

Letter of Viscount Mountstuart, envoy at Turin, to Robert Liston, 20 December 1782.

32 × 45 cm

*BL Department of Manuscripts
Add. MS 36804, ff. 17-25*

Lord Mountstuart broke his journey in Paris on 16 December 1782, and there obtained detailed intelligence of the signing of the Preliminary Articles of Peace on 30 November 1782. He dismisses the story that Franklin had donned a special coat for the occasion (a slander later contradicted by Whitefoord in the London press). He corrects at the end of the letter his statement about the British signatories being

Fitzherbert and Oswald: 'I am mistaken . . . Oswald signed alone under a Commission from the great Seal. Strachy & Fitzherbert had a power from the King to consent to the article respecting the fishery which they have under their hand.'

John Stuart, Viscount Mountstuart, the eldest son of Lord Bute, George III's intimate friend, used his diplomatic facilities for travel for undertaking in 1782-83 a series of unofficial personal ventures in peace-making.

**172 Publication in London, 1783**

Provisional Articles, Signed at Paris, the 30th of November, 1782, by the Commissioner of His Britannic Majesty, and the Commissioners of the United States of America. Published by Authority. London: Printed for T. Harrison and S. Brooke, 1783.

34 cm

*BL Department of Printed Books
BS 68/79 (1)*

The published text of the Provisional Articles omitted the secret Separate Article concerning West Florida, appended to the original document and never ratified. The Treaty between Spain and Great Britain whereby Great Britain yielded both East and West Florida to Spain had made this Article unnecessary.

**173 Signing the Preliminary Articles of Peace, 20 January 1783**

The Preliminary Articles of Peace between Great Britain & France and Great Britain and Spain, signed at Versailles Jan.ʸ 20 1783 by Mr. Fitzherbert . . . Hamilton delin. Pollard sculp.

Engraved for Barnard's New Complete and Authentic History of England.

32 × 22 cm

*BL Department of Printed Books
Cup. 1247.cc.17*

170

The Preliminary Articles of Peace between Great Britain and America were to be made into a treaty only when the terms of peace between Great Britain and France and Spain had been settled. The Count de Vergennes, French Foreign Minister, had professed himself amazed to learn that the American and British Commissioners had signed separately and secretly on 30 November 1782, to the exclusion of France. The preliminary treaties between Great Britain and France and Great Britain and Spain were both signed on 20 January 1783, Alleyne Fitzherbert signing for Great Britain, Gravier de Vergennes for France, and the Conde d'Aranda for Spain. The Preliminary Treaty with the Dutch was not signed until September 1783.

174(a)

## 174 Declaration for the Cessation of Hostilities

*Lent by the Public Record Office*
F.O.93/8/1, F.O. 94/1.

The declarations for the suspension of arms and Cessation of Hostilities between Great Britain and the United States made on 20 January 1783 were part of the general scheme of an armistice and a peace for all belligerents. They were signed concurrently with the Preliminary Articles of Peace between Great Britain and France and Great Britain and Spain. Following this, the American commissioners, Adams, Franklin and Jay, signed a declaration (in substance a proclamation) of peace at Paris on 20 February 1783, the single original of which is illustrated. The Articles of Peace were then ratified by the United States on 15 April 1783 (F.O. 94/1). Their instrument of ratification served as a proclamation of the text. It was signed by Elias Boudinet, President of Congress, and Robert R. Livingstone, Secretary for Foreign Affairs, and attested by Charles Thomson, Secretary. The approval of Congress, given on 11 April, was not a formal ratification.

against his said Majesty, the King of Great Britain, or his Subjects under the Penalty of incurring the highest Displeasure of the said United States.

Given at Paris the Twentieth Day of February, in the Year of our Lord, one Thousand, Seven hundred and Eighty Three; under our Hands and Seals

John Adams

Franklin

John Jay

174(b)

**175 Peace between Great Britain and the United States of America, September 1783**

The Definitive Treaty of Peace and Friendship between His Britannick Majesty, and the United States of America. Signed at Paris, the 3d of September, 1783. Published by Authority. London: Printed by T. Harrison and S. Brooke, 1783.

23cm

*BL Department of Printed Books* 816.l.50(3)

On Wednesday 3 September 1783, the definitive treaty between Great Britain and the United States of America was signed at David Hartley's apartments in the Hôtel d'York in Paris. As Minister Plenipotentiary representing a crowned head, Hartley signed first for Great Britain, the names of Adams, Franklin and Jay following. The Treaty differed from the Preliminary Articles only in the omission of the secret Article and the addition of Article X, granting six months for formal ratification.

On the same day the Duke of Manchester signed the treaties with France and Spain at Versailles.

**176 The Map of the Treaty 1782**

A Map of the British Colonies in North America with the Roads, Distances, Limits, and Extent of the settlements, Humbly Inscribed to the Right Honourable the Earl of Halifax . . . By . . . Jnº Mitchell. Tho: Kitchin Sculp. London: Publish'd by the Author, 1755 [1775]. MS additions by Richard Oswald, *c.*1782.

1:2,000,000. 197 × 140cm

*BL Department of Printed Books* K.118.*d*.26 (*K. Top. CXVIII* 49.*b*)

The Red-lined Map, known also as 'King George's Map', records (in its MS additions) the official British interpretation of the negotiations at Paris, as concluded in the Preliminary Articles of Peace, 1782. The red line, defined as 'The Boundary as described by Mr. Oswald', marks the limits of the United States and her neighbours. This and other annotations are in Richard Oswald's hand. Other boundaries indicate (1) conflicting interpretations of the Treaty of Utrecht, as seen by Great Britain and France; (2) boundaries of territories granted to the Hudson Bay Company; (3) boundaries of the Province of Quebec defined in 1763 and 1774; (4) boundaries of the areas included in Indian Lands, as defined by Royal Proclamation, 1763.

The base map is the fifth edition (1775) of John Mitchell's map of North America, first published in 1755 with the title 'A Map of the British and French Dominions in North America', and regarded by most authorities as the finest map of North America of its day. Oswald had brought the map to the council table, as Franklin records in a letter to Thomas Jefferson, 8 April 1790, discussing alleged Canadian incroachments: 'I am perfectly clear in the remembrance that the map we used in tracing the boundary, was brought to the treaty by the commissioners from England, and that it was the same that was published by Mitchell about twenty years before. . . . That the map we used was Mitchell's map, Congress were acquainted at the time, by a letter to their Secretary for Foreign Affairs, which I suppose may be found upon their files.' This map appears to have been prepared as the official copy for the King, and came to the British Museum in 1828 in King George III's Topographical Collection.

For Colour Plate, see p.96

**177 Portraits of the Peace-makers**

1: Benjamin Franklin (1706–90)
(a) An oval medallion of Benjamin Franklin (1706–90). Bust in profile facing left on blue ground. Impressed: Franklin.

*BM Department of Medieval and Later Antiquities, Pottery Catalogue I. 74*

177(1c)

*Caleb Whitefoord*

177(4)

One of Wedgwood's series of large portraits, the 'Illustrious Moderns', showing Franklin in classical style. No less than eight different portraits of Franklin were produced by Wedgwood between 1775 and 1790.

(c) Benjamin Franklin et vita inter Americanos acta, et magnis electricitatis periculis clarus.
   J. Elias Haid sculp, 1780.

   23 × 14cm

*BM Department of Prints and Drawings*
1877-8-11-842

One of the most popular portraits of Benjamin Franklin was the 'fur cap' print. Engraved by Augustin de Saint Aubin after a drawing by Charles Nicholas Cochin, the original was published on the occasion of Franklin's earlier diplomatic mission to Paris in 1777. The fur cap, acquired on a journey to Canada in 1776 and worn indoors and out during Franklin's first winter in Paris, had made a sensation among the delighted Parisians. It was reported that ladies were dressing their hair 'à la Franklin'.

The English engraving of 1780 by J. Elias Haid, one of many derived versions, has a Latin text in which Franklin's political achievements and electrical inventions are neatly blended.

2: John Jay, appointed American Minister-Plenipotentiary to Spain, 1779. R. Wilkinson, London, 1783.

3: John Adams, Puritan from Braintree, Mass., appointed by Congress to negotiate peace with Great Britain, 1781. D. Kennedy, Philadelphia.

4: Caleb Whitefoord, Secretary to the British Commission. Portrait by Geo. Dance, 6 July 1795. Wm. Daniel Fecit. London 1809.

5: Charles Gravier, Comte de Vergennes, French Foreign Minister: Gravé par Clément Bervie. 1780.

(b) An oval medallion: bust in profile facing left on blue ground. Impressed mark on back: WEDGWOOD & BENTLEY.

   Height 10¾ in, 27cm

*BM Medieval and Later Antiquities*
1909, 12-1, 149

*Charles Gravier* *Comte de Vergennes*
*Commandeur des* *Ordres du Roi,*
*Conseiller d'Etat d'Epée,* *Ministre et Secret.<sup>re</sup> d'Etat*
*ayant le Département* *des affaires étrangères.*

*Dessiné d'après Nature et Gravé par Clement Pierre en 1780.*

177(5)

EUROPEAN MAGAZINE.

*M. Griffiths del.*      *Corner sculp.*

*Count de Florida Blanca.*

*Publish'd by J. Sewell, 32, Cornhill, Jan. 1. 1791.*

177(6)

6: Count de Florida Blanca, Spanish Foreign Minister:
M. Griffiths del. Corner sculp. London, 1791.
From the *European Magazine*.

**178 Farewell to John Jay, 1784**

Letter from Richard Oswald to Caleb White-foord signed and dated Friday evening 7 o'clock. [May 1784.]

25 × 20cm

*BL Department of Manuscripts*
*Add. MS 36595, f.198*

John Jay, John Adams and Henry Laurens were in London in 1784 (thereby providing the opportunity for Benjamin West to paint his group portrait). With Jay, his wife and family at Dover about to depart for New York in company with Laurens, Oswald invites Whitefoord to join the farewell party, 'believing it not likely that we shall have another meeting on this side [of] the great Lake'.

**179 Caleb Whitefoord's Services to Peace Go Unrewarded, 1785**

Letter from Benjamin Franklin at Passy to Caleb Whitefoord in London, 19 May 1785.

23 × 19cm

*BL Department of Manuscripts*
*Add. MS 36593, ff. 210-211*

'My dear old Friend . . . I am really griev'd to learn by your Letter to my Grandson, that your public Services at the Treaty remain yet un-rewarded . . . it is a shame you should be so long neglected. The Ministry being chang'd does not lessen your Merit with regard to the Public. You had a great Loss in the Death of that truly good Man Mr Oswald: For I know it was his Inten-tion . . . to make it a Point with Government, the obtaining of a handsome Provision for you.'

Whitefoord had to wait for due recompense until April 1790, when he received £400 for his services at Paris, and on 20 July 1793 he was granted a pension of £200 a year.

## 180 Whitefoord is Elected to the American Philosophical Society, 1790

To all Persons to whom these Presents shall come, Greeting. The American Philosophical Society held at Philadelphia . . . have elected Caleb Whitefoord Esq.r a Member . . . In testimony whereof the said Society have caused the seal of their Corporation to be annexed to this Certificate, 14 February 1791.

30 × 44cm

*BL Department of Manuscripts*
*Add. MS 36593, f. 269*

To the news of his election on 15 January 1790 as a member of the American Philosophical Society Whitefoord replied: 'Nothing could be more agreeable to me. . . . Your venerated President, the late Dr. Benjamin Franklin, had for many years honoured me with his Friendship; and perhaps that Intimacy, which was the Pride and the Happiness of my Life, may have in some Degree recommended me to your Notice.' He continues: 'I have long been a sincere Wellwisher to America, and no one lamented more the unhappy Quarrel between the Colonies and the Parent State: And having lent a helping hand to stop the Horrors of War, & to negociate a Peace . . . I have the Satisfaction to think, that I have not lived in vain.'

## 181 Parliament debates American Independence, 9 July 1782

A Complete and Accurate Account of the Very Important Debate in the House of Commons on Tuesday July 9, 1782. London: Sold by J. Stockdale, 1782.

20cm

*BL Department of Printed Books, T318.(3.)*

The following debate (writes the publisher) is universally allowed to be the most important one that ever happened in the House of Commons. General Conway, continuing in office under Lord Shelburne after the resignation of Fox, recommends as the policy of the Ministry that the independence of America should be acknowledged, and that this should be done in order to bring about peace. 'America ought to be declared independent rather than that this country should be undone.'

## 182 King George III's proclamation of peace, 1783

(a) A Proclamation, declaring the Cessation of Arms, as well by Sea as Land, agreed upon between His Majesty, the Most Christian King, the King of Spain, the States General of the United Provinces, and the United States of America; In: *The London Gazette* numb. 12414. Feb 11 – Feb 15 1783.

18 × 30cm

*BL Official Publications Library O.G.E. 70*

A Minute of the Cabinet Meeting held on 24 January 1783 at Lord Grantham's office humbly submitted that His Majesty should ratify the Preliminary Articles of Peace signed at Versailles on 20 January. The King's proclamation, 'given at Our Court at St. James the 14th day of February 1783' concludes: 'We declare, That Our Royal Will and Pleasure is, and we do hereby strictly charge and command all Our Officers both at Sea and Land and all other Our Subjects whatsoever, to forbear all Acts of Hostility either by Sea or Land, against His Most Christian Majesty, the King of Spain, the States General of the United Provinces and the United States of America.'

The proclamation was also issued in New York as a broadside.

(b) Proclamation of Peace.
Pub.d Oc.r 21st 1783, by W. Wells, No 132, Fleet Street.

Engraving 32 × 26cm

*BM Department of Prints and Drawings, Satires 6267*

The TEA-TAX-TEMPEST. or OLD TIME with his MAGICK=LANTHERN.

*Pb.ᵈ March 12 1783. by W. Humphreys. Nᵒ 227 Strand.*

12. Mar. 1783.

183

### 183 The Tea-Tax-Tempest, 1783.

The Tea-Tax-Tempest or Old Time with his
Magick-Lanthern. Published March 12 1783
by W. Humphreys Nᵒ 227 Strand.

Engraving.

26 × 36cm

*BM Department of Prints and Drawings,
Satires* 6190

This cartoon is a reduced and altered copy of a
German cartoon, 'The Tea-Tax-Tempest, or
the Anglo-American Revolution', 1778 (*Satires*
5490) which in its turn was an adaptation in
reverse of 'The Oracle' by John Dixon, published in 1774 (*Satires* 5225). The chief alteration
in this new version is the large white label
issuing from the mouth of Time, describing the
scene projected 'There you see the little Hot
Spit Fire Tea pot that has done all the Mis-
chief . . .'

The snake emblem on the American flag had
been designed in 1754 by Benjamin Franklin for
the *Pennsylvania Gazette*. After the first Congress in 1774 this was superseded by a living
snake encircling a tree or the staff of liberty.
The snake was a useful symbol for British
cartoonists to seize upon with the obvious con-
notation of American treacherous behaviour.
'There you see thirteen Stripes and Rattle-
Snake exalted . . .'

184

*ENGLAND'S SUN SETTING*

PEACE — PEACE — P-E-A-C

AMERICA

ATLANTIC

'Alas poor Country, almost afraid to know itself'. — Macbeth.

THE BLESSINGS OF PEACE.

Publish'd according to Act of Parliament by M. Smith in Fleet Street. April 16th 1783.

1. Dr Franklin  5. D. of Richmond  9. The —  13. Mr Pitt
2. K. of Spain  6. Ld Shelburne  10. Lord Mansfield  14. Lord Nugent
3. K. of France  7. Edmund Burke  11. Mr Sheridan  15. Lord Keppel
Charles Fox  8. Lord Thurlow  12. Lord North  16. Ld Ashburton
17. Lord Amherst

## 184 The Blessings of Peace, 1783

The Blessings of Peace. Publish'd according to Act of Parliament by M. Smith in Fleet Street April 16 1783.

Coloured engraving. 32 × 39cm

*BM Department of Prints and Drawings, Satires* 6212

On the left in America a young Indian girl representing the USA sits between Spain and France, giving a hand to each, while Benjamin Franklin crowns her with a wreath. In England a crowd of politicians stand around the King who asks anxiously 'My Lords and Gentlemen, what should I do?' They offer diverse and conflicting advice, reflecting the disarray defeat had brought to English politics. On the left of the group Charles Fox stamps his foot shouting 'Keep Peace on any Terms', while Lord North standing before the King mutters unhappily, 'I thought to have had America at our Feet, but I see tis otherwise.' In the sky riding on a broomstick is a witch in a cloak and steeple-crowned hat, behind her are black clouds, across which streams a label coming from beneath her petticoats, inscribed 'Peace – Peace P-E-A-C'. Behind the hill is 'England's sun setting'.

### 185 Public Thanksgiving, 1784

By the King. A Proclamation for a Publick Thanksgiving. London, Charles Eyre and William Strachan, Printers to the King's most Excellent Majesty, 1784.

*BL Official Publications Library B.J.5 (187)*

'Whereas it has pleased Almighty God ... to put an End to the late Bloody, Extended, and Expensive War ... We therefore ... have thought fit ... to issue this Our Royal Proclamation, hereby appointing and commanding, that a General Thanksgiving be observed ... on Thursday, the Twenty-ninth Day of this instant July ...

'Given at our Court at St. James's the Second day of July 1784.'

### 186 Letters of King George III, 1782–83

*Royal Library, Windsor, lent by Gracious Permission of Her Majesty Queen Elizabeth II.*

The King writing to Lord Shelburne from Windsor on 10 November 1782, at 6.55 pm, says: 'I cannot conclude without mentioning how sensibly I feel the dismemberment of America from this Empire ...' The King finds some small consolation in the thought that 'knavery seems to be so much the striking feature of its Inhabitants that it may not in the end be an evil that they become Aliens to this Kingdom.' The King writing to Lord North from Windsor on 7 September 1783, at 5.44 pm, says: 'I have signed the Warrant for the Attendance of the Heralds for the Proclamation of Peace. ... I am glad it is on a day I am not in Town, as I think this compleats the Downfall of the lustre of this Empire.'

RA 5051, 5617. Printed by Fortescue, nos. 3978 and 4470.

### 187 King George III (1738–1820)

Oval medallion: impressed mark on back: WEDGWOOD.

Height: 3½in. 9cm
*BM Department of Medieval and Later Antiquities*

1909, 12-1, 134

Bust in profile facing right on blue ground. Remodelled by William Hackwood 1776 from his earlier model adapted from a wax portrait by Isaac Gosset.

### 188 Reports in the London Press

*BL Department of Printed Books, Burney Newspapers*

*Morning Chronicle, and London Advertiser*, no. 4287, 12 February 1783: Genuine Letters from Gentlemen of Character in New-York, Nov. 8 1782. 'People's fears still continue, that this place will be abandoned next spring, and Independency granted to America. ... Giving up New-York will be virtually giving up all America at once.' (Burney 723b)

*Morning Chronicle and London Advertiser*, no. 4489, 6 October 1783: Ceremonial for the Proclamation of Peace, this day, October 6, 1783. Extract of a letter from Newburgh, 24 June 1783, from General Washington to the President of Congress. (Burney 733b)

*The Whitehall Evening Post*, no. 5548, 25 January 1783: [extract from] *Pennsylvania Gazette* of 11 November. 'A discovery has lately been made on this Continent that will astonish the whole world. Our great and excellent General Washington is actually discovered to be of the female sex.' (Burney 739b)

### 189 Letter from George Washington, 1783

A circular Letter from George Washington, Commander in Chief of the Armies of the United States of America, to His Excellency William Greene, Esq., Governor of the State of Rhode Island. London, J. Stockdale, 1783.

20cm

*BL Department of Printed Books 8132.e.65*

About to retire into private life, Washington makes this last official communication, to congratulate the Governor on 'the glorious events which Heaven has been pleased to produce in our favour'. The citizens of America are placed in the most enviable condition, as the sole Lords and proprietors of a vast tract of continent, comprehending all the various soils and elements of the world. It is now left to the United States to show whether they will be respectable and prosperous, or contemptible and miserable, as a nation. This is the moment, when the eyes of the whole world are turned upon them to establish or ruin their national character for ever.

This letter was designed as an appendix to the pamphlet *Addresses and Recommendations of Congress to the United States of America* (1783).

### 190 Charleston receives news from New York, Philadelphia and London

*South Carolina Gazette, and General Advertiser.* Tuesday 3 June 1783. Vol 1. numb. 29.

*BL Department of Printed Books C. 42.l.1(2)*

It is reported from Philadelphia that the flag of the Thirteen United States of America has been grossly insulted in New York, which was not evacuated by the British until November 1783. Charles Logie is appointed British ambassador to the United States. News from London reports 'a spirit of mutiny and discontent . . . throughout the kingdom, particularly the soldiery and much so on board the ships of war, for the want of their pay'.

### 191 News of Peace Reaches New York, 1783

25 March 1783. Published by James Rivington, Printer to the King's Most Excellent Majesty. (A facsimile, 1898)

38 × 30cm

*BL Department of Printed Books 1865.c.7.(12)*

Report of the arrival of an Express from New Jersey, bringing an account of the Preliminaries to a general peace between Great Britain, France, Spain, Holland and the United States of America, signed at Paris. Hostilities are to cease in Europe on 20 February, and in America on 20 March, 1783. 'This very *important* Intelligence was last night announced by the Firing of

Cannon, and great Rejoicings at Elizabeth-Town.'

### 192 George Washington requests British military withdrawal from America

Letter from George Washington to General Haldimand. Signed and dated from Headquarters on Hudson River 12 July 1783.

19 × 38cm

*BL Department of Manuscripts Add. MS 21835, ff. 174-175*

In implementation of Article VII of the Preliminary Articles of Peace, Washington has been instructed by Congress to arrange with the Commander-in-Chief of the British forces in America for receiving the posts and fortresses still occupied by British troops; he requests General Haldimand, Commander-in-Chief in Canada, to receive Washington's envoy, Baron de Steuben, who is to make a tour of the frontier area in the region of the St Lawrence and Great Lakes. Article VII required the King 'to withdraw all His Armies, Garrisons and Fleets from the . . . United States, and from every Port, Place and Harbour within the same'.

### 193 General Haldimand's Reply

Letter of Haldimand to Washington, 11 August 1783

34 × 42cm

*BL Department of Manuscripts Add. MS 21835 ff.193-4*

Haldimand replies that 'His Majesty's Proclamation declaring a Cessation of Hostilities with the Powers at War, and particular Orders to comply with it, are the only Instructions I have yet received upon the important Subject of Peace'. He has therefore to defer compliance with Washington's requests until properly authorized to receive them. He assures Washington that his officers serving in the Upper Country have been 'unweariedly employed in restraining the Indians, and reconciling them to Peace'.

**194 Peace in Pennsylvania, 1784**

By the President and the Supreme Executive Council of the Commonwealth of Pennsylvania, A Proclamation. 22 January 1784.

44 × 38cm

*BL Department of Manuscripts*
*Add. MS 21835, ff. 211-2*

The Definitive Articles of Peace, as concluded and signed on 3 September 1783, are made known to the citizens of Pennsylvania, who are charged and commanded to observe and act conformable to the same. Sheriffs are to make the Proclamation public in their respective counties. The signatures of John Dickinson and John Armstrong appear in the margins. This copy was probably sent to Haldimand by the Chevalier de la Luzerne, French Minister in Philadelphia, who was corresponding with Haldimand before his departure for France.

**195 The British Withdrawal from New York**

Letter from Governor George Clinton to General Haldimand signed and dated 19 March 1784.

20 × 32cm

*BL Department of Manuscripts*
*Add. MS 21835, f. 221*

As required by Article VII of the Treaty, George Clinton, Governor of New York, requests the withdrawal of the British garrisons under Haldimand's command from the Post of Niagara and other posts now within the United States, in the State of New York.

**196 Resettling the Indian Nations, 1784**

A meeting held at Niagara 22nd May 1784 with the Mississaga Indians accompanied by the Chiefs and Warriors of the Six Nations Delawares &c.

30 × 19cm

*BL Department of Manuscripts*
*Add. MS 21835, ff. 231-2*

At the great Council Tree, Lieut.-Col. John Butler asks the Mississaga Indians to give up land between the Lakes Ontario, Huron and Erie, for the settlement of Indians of the Six Nations who had fought as Loyalists in the War and now had to be resettled in Canada. Pokquan, Mississaga Speaker, answers in agreement: 'We are Indians, and consider ourselves and the Six Nations to be one and the same people, and agreeable to a former, and mutual agreement, we are bound to help each other.'

**197 Settlement of the Loyalists in Quebec**

Estimate of the Quantity of Lands that may be required to settle the K.R.R. New York . . . and Refugee Loyalists in the Province of Quebec.

33 × 20cm

*BL Department of Manuscripts*
*Add. MS 21829, ff. 62-3*

By 1782 the entire company of loyalist refugees in America were concentrated in New York. Early in 1782 bands began to leave New York for Nova Scotia, Quebec and Upper Canada. Haldimand as Governor of Quebec had to organize these operations of resettlement. This document estimates a total requirement of 483,840 acres for the settlement of the New York militia and Loyalists.

**198 The Fate of the Loyalists**

The Savages let loose, or the cruel Fate of the Loyalists. March 1783. W. Humphrey.

21 × 33 cm

*BM Department of Prints and Drawings,*
*Satires 6182*

The cartoonist shows American loyalists being murdered by Red Indians. In fact, the chief danger to the Loyalists was not from Red Indians but from American Patriots. The British peace negotiators had obtained for the Loyalists the best terms possible in the compromise set out in Article V of the Preliminary Articles of Peace.

*Is this a Peace, when Loyalists must bleed?*  The SAVAGES let loose, OR  *It is a Bloody Piece of work indeed.*
The Cruel FATE of the LOYALISTS.

198

## 199 The Settlement of Upper Canada

Elizabeth Simcoe's birchbark map of Upper Canada, 1794-96.

19 × 29cm

*BL Map Library K. Top. CXIX. 15*

The settlement of the Loyalists in Upper Canada brought about the establishment of a new province, Upper Canada, of which General Simcoe was appointed the first governor in 1791. His wife accompanied her husband on his travels, recording the scene in thirty-one views of Upper Canada, and a map which shows the governor's projected towns, and proposed and existing military roads.

## 200 The United States of America, 1783

The United States of North America with the British and Spanish Territories according to the Treaty. Engrav'd by Wm. Faden 1783.

53 × 92cm

*BL Map Library 184.i.3(3)*

One of the earliest maps to name and depict the United States, this was issued by Faden as a revised version of his map 'The British Colonies in North America, 1777'. The first issue of the map in 1783 showed two rivers named St Croix running into Passamaquoddy Bay in the Bay of Fundy. In this second issue of the same year the name St Croix has been suppressed on the more westerly of the two rivers. This copy of the map has a detailed MS sketch of the critical area attached. As the St Croix river was agreed as the frontier between Nova Scotia and the United States, the problem of its identification was a vital one. Following the discovery that the Mitchell map was inaccurate in its depiction of the St Croix River, an arbitration commission, the Saint Croix Commission, 1796-98, had to be set up to settle this territorial problem.

### 201 An Englishman visits the new republic, 1784

Letter from Thomas Mullett to John Wilkes, 15 February 1784, written from Charleston, South Carolina.
*BL Department of Manuscripts*
*Add. MS 30872, ff. 239-40*

'I have travelld from Portsmouth in New Hampshire, to Savannah in Georgia. . . . South of Pennsylvania thro Maryland, Virginia, North Carolina, South Carolina & Georgia the people are more thinly scatter'd, and from the savage manner in which the War was conducted, their Resentment against the English is yet very powerful. The epithets of *the Enemy* and *the British* are universally in use, and they are sometimes so expressd, even by the mildest dispositions, in the Recital of events, as to prove that hatred has supplanted Respect & esteem. . . . Whilst the present generation lives Cornwallis, Rawdon, Balfour, Tarlton, & Craig will never be forgotten.'

Despite the bitter feelings about the War, Mullett sees great prospects for British trade: 'it will be the fault of England if she does not secure to herself the benefits of the most valuable part of the Trade of this Country. . . . The groundwork must be a *Conciliatory temper*, and a *liberal Commercial System*.' Finally, Mullett is so impressed with New York that he tells Wilkes 'were you Prime Minister instead of Chamberlain I should be almost tempted to sollicit the Consulship at your hands'.

# Select Reading List

Some general works relating to aspects of the period 1763–83:

ALDEN, JOHN R. *The American Revolution, 1775–83*. New York, 1954.

BAILYN, BERNARD ed. *Pamphlets of the American Revolution, 1750–1776*. Cambridge, Mass., 1965– .

BETTS, C. W. *American colonial history illustrated by contemporary medals. . .* Edited, with notes, by William T. R. Marvin . . . and Lyman Haynes Low. New York, 1894.

CARTER, C. E. *The correspondence of General Thomas Gage with the Secretaries of State 1763–75*. New Haven, 1931, 2 Vols.

CHRISTIE, I. R. *Wilkes, Wyvill and Reform: The parliamentary reform movement*, New York, 1962.
— *Crisis of Empire: Great Britain and the American colonies*, London, 1966.

COLONIAL SOCIETY OF MASSACHUSETTS. *Boston prints and printmakers 1670–1775*. Boston, 1973.

COMMAGER, H. S. ed. *The spirit of 'Seventy-Six*. New York, 1958, 2 Vols.

DICKERSON, OLIVER M. *The Navigation Acts and the American Revolution*. Philadelphia, 1951; repr. New York, 1973.

FORTESCUE, SIR JOHN, ed. *The correspondence of King George the Third 1760–1783*. London, 1927–8, 6 Vols.

GIPSON, L. H. *The British Empire before the American Revolution*. Vols. IX–XII, New York, 1961–65.

HIGGINBOTHAM, DON. *The War of American Independence. Military attitudes, policies and practice, 1763–87*, New York and London, 1971.

KNOLLENBERG, BERNARD. *Origins of the American Revolution 1759–66*. New York, 1960.

LAMB, R. *An original and authentic journal of occurrences during the late American War from its commencement to the year 1783*. Dublin, 1809.

MACKESY, P. *The War for America 1775–1783*. London, 1964.

MORGAN, E. S. and MORGAN, H. M. *The Stamp Act Crisis, 1764–66*. Chapel Hill, 1953.

MORRIS, R. B. *The peace makers: the great powers and American independence*. New York, 1965.

NEBENZAHL, KENNETH and HIGGINBOTHAM, DON. *Atlas of the American Revolution*. Chicago, 1974.

ROSS, CHARLES. *Correspondence of Charles, First Marquis Cornwallis*. London, 1859. 3 Vols.

SATIRES *Catalogue of prints and drawings in the British Museum. Division I. Political and personal satires*. Vol IV, 1761–70. Prepared by F. G. Stephens. London, 1883.

— *Catalogue of political and personal satires preserved in the Departments of Prints and Drawings in the British Museum*. Vol V, 1771–83. By M. D. George. London, 1935.

WRIGHT, ESMOND. *Fabric of Freedom, 1763–1800*. New York, 1961.

WRIGHT, ESMOND. *A tug of loyalties. Anglo-American relations 1765–85*. London, 1975.